Endless Summer

Inspirations and Reflections
for the Journey to Life Balance

Halleemah Nash

Editor: Precious Shalom Williams

Back Cover Photo: Jason McCoy, Jason McCoy Photography

Marketing and Design: Kristin Williams, FAME Production Group

Copyright © 2014 Halleemah Nash

All rights reserved.

ISBN-13: 978-1495908712

DEDICATION

This book is dedicated to my mentors who have closely shaped the woman I am today - Robert L. Nash, Michele Chambers, Josephine Ruffin, Gail Jackson, Linda Webb, Lisa Yeboah, and Frances Wright. I pray that this book helps someone the way you all have so intricately helped me to create balance in my life.

PRAISE FOR ENDLESS SUMMER

Most devotionals are bland, generic and stale. Endless Summer actually motivates you to press forward into the life that God has planned for you. This would be a great resource for small groups, early morning prayer, or anyone else looking to be inspired.
DJ Wade-O
Founder, Wade-O Radio & Christian Hip Hop Media Innovator

Nash writes with such humble transparency that you are immediately drawn in. The meditations are altogether helpful, and most importantly, Gospel-centered, with tools for application in life's harder seasons.
JP Chookaszian
Social Entrepreneur & Co-Founder, Urban Offering

Endless Summer reminds me that, I can speak truth to all my dreams, and creating a life worth living is impossible without the Word of God.
Alicia Graf Mack
Lead Dancer, Alvin Ailey American Dance Theatre

With clarity and light, Halleemah's inspired reflections have the power to translate scriptural lessons and principles to a generation of skeptics and seekers. Her personal transparency is refreshing and grounding, yet always pointing the reader back to the Eternal Truth. Her voice is needed and necessary...a bridge for this generation!
Michael McBride,
Social Activist & Senior Pastor, The Way Christian Center

We need more conductors. Halleemah Nash is definitely one of the foremost role models and conductors for truth and success for today's young girls.
Kelly Fair
Founder, Polished Pebbles Girls Mentorship Program

This book is so relatable. For some reason, it feels "cool" to read. She made me feel Kendrick's "Sing About Me…Dying of Thirst" in my soul! Even if you don't usually buy devotionals, this is one to get!
Kendall Hurns
Owner, Robotic Minds Clothing

Inspiring, encouraging and practical, each devotional hit home for me and gave me a take away perspective that I hadn't independently considered.
Loni Swain
Radio Personality, WGCI Chicago

TABLE OF CONTENTS

Introduction	11
Distractions in Your To Do List	17
Rejection as a Tool	20
#TeamNoSleep	23
Label-less…Limitless…Synonyms	26
Forgiving Our Fathers	29
Housebuilding 101	32
Stay in Your Lane	35
Frontin'	38
Get Focused	41
Conquering King	44
Don't Be a Hater	47
The Hope Dealer	50
Prayer	53
The Pity Party Does Not Turn Up	56
Slingshot Practice On Hilltop High	59
Praying For Our Exes	62
Fearless You…	65
Winery Revelations	68
Replay	71
Your Design Is On Purpose	74
Disruption of the Statistics	77
"No" Is a Complete Sentence	80
Sing About Me	83

TABLE OF CONTENTS

Vision Boarding	86
Purple Heart	89
Fail Better	92
Deepened Gratitude	95
Discipline in Money Management	98
Each One Reach One	101
Rest in God's Complete Care	104
Leadership Intercession	107
How Foolish Of Me	110
Leadership in the Workplace	113
Fashioned in Vintage	116
A World Worthy Of Its Children	119
Ready? Set? Chill.	122
Feng Shui Your Friendships	124
Devo for the Traveler Bee	127
Re-Imagine Suffering	130
Worth the Wait	133
Salty- Release from Our Past	135
Encouragement for the Middle	138
Fasting and Prayer	141
Don't Sweat the Technique	144
Power of Presence	147
Time Mindfulness	150
Epilogue	154

INTRODUCTION

The summertime is without question my favorite season of the year. I am a California child, so I adore sunshine, beach days, outdoors activities, waking up jovial to the sunrise, and the constant motivation that comes with being solar powered. Consequently, my least favorite season is the winter. I literally despise being cold. During winter months, I experience lulls in productivity, I rarely go outdoors, I am extremely non-social, and I find myself sad in gloomy and dark weather.

Chicago, Illinois, where I currently reside, recently experienced one of its worst winters in decades. A winter storm toppled the city with record-breaking snowfall and similar winter storms were also seen throughout the midwest, northeast and in a number of southern cities. At the top of the year it was reported that Chicago had endured the third snowiest January since 1884 when snowfall started being recorded. It was a long and brutal winter, especially for someone who struggles to find a consistent level of joy, peace, and productivity in the colder months. It was in the eye of this winter storm that I wrote these pages.

During this storm, I spent some time reflecting on the idea of balance and not living in extremes. My gravitation toward summer became a perfect analogy for what I'd hoped to accomplish in my quest toward a greater equilibrium in my life.

My search for balance was a search for consistent joy and gratefulness, along with an endless season of light. Light, joy, and gratefulness were all available to me in the winter just as they were in the summer. However, the discomfort of the season made it difficult to see this clearly.

This book is a collection of reflections that I wrote on my journey toward an Endless Summer. In other words, this book is a journaling and recap of critical lessons I learned in my quest for balance. The journey to trust God through inconvenient and uncomfortable seasons is my pursuit to have the same level of energy and excitement for life through periods that feel like cold winters. In truth, we all have found ourselves considering balance at some point. We all search for how we might accomplish consistency in our faith, hope, and joy in spite of life's circumstances that seem to oppose this effort. How do we find streams in the middle of life's deserts? How do we find the solace of peace in the midst of life's storms? As I pondered these questions I learned that the answers were intimately connected to my perspective and my determination to embrace the understanding that every season has a specific blessing.

Although I share a number of personal stories along the way, this is not a memoir. This is a compilation of illustrations and narratives that reveal the healing and development of my perspective throughout my Christian journey. I discovered a deeper level of gratefulness and freedom in the Lord once I embraced the truth that within my own perspective lay my blueprint to balance.

Balance is more than the management of how many hours we spend at work and at home. It is more than task lists, vacation time, and committing to balancing actionable activities. Balance is also connected to outlook and perspective. It is connected to our own ability to let go, forgive, see God's creation in every day, and the right definition of failure and trials. How do I understand faith? Am I committed to a prayer life? What kinds of things weigh me down and hinder my ability to be grateful when life hands me difficult challenges? How do I remain strong when my flesh is weak? What limiting soul prisons have I built? How do I think outside of the boxes that society has created for me? How can I be grateful in my current season without coveting the next one in an unhealthy way? How do I embrace God's acceptance of me as I am but still constantly strive for holy living? How do I know God, as Paul said, in both the fellowship of His suffering and the power of His resurrection? The key to answering these questions is discovering a balanced perspective.

I do not wear the crown of a balanced life. We are all constantly growing and balance is something I too am working toward. But, for the first time, the fierce Chicago winter was not as debilitating to me. These reflections were my intentional exercise in producing and embodying light along the backdrop of what has historically been an undesirable season. I gave winter a brand new name and it will be forever changed in my outlook.

This doesn't mean that you will find me ice-skating during snowfall or frolicking outside in the face of wind chill. What it does mean is that I have now developed a loving relationship with uncomfortable periods of time. There is something great that can be produced in the midst of discomfort. As a matter of fact, I would argue that it is where God produces His greatest work. It is in fire where gold is purified, and in pressure where coals become diamonds. And, it is in the winter where I found my balance. What's your winter? How will you rename it? I pray that you might be built, encouraged, and developed through this book and that you too, will discover more consistent seasons of balance.

In the midst of winter, I found there was, within me, an invincible summer. And that makes me happy. For it says that no matter how hard the world pushes against me, within me, there's something stronger – something better, pushing right back.

Albert Camus, The Stranger

DISTRACTIONS IN THE DETAILS

"Martha, Martha," the Lord answered, "you are worried and upset about many things, but few things are needed– or indeed only one. Mary has chosen what is better, and it will not be taken away from her."

Luke 10:41-42, NIV

My life is often managed by my daily tasks or what is affectionately labeled my "To Do" list. It is how I ensure that I accomplish and track the multiplicity of responsibilities attached to being both a minister and business owner. I, like many others, have often lost myself in the duties of the day. Whether it's an executive, an entrepreneur, a student with a part time job, or a working parent, today's millennial is constantly charged with learning new ways to be effective at the art of multitasking. Like Martha, our concurrent lives are vulnerable to the threat of being easily distracted. So much so that our tasks lists, calendars, emails and social media messaging garner more attention than the scripture passages that would grant us strength for these tasks.

The bible illustrates that while Mary sits at Jesus' feet, Martha is anxious and overly concerned with the details of Jesus' visit to their home. Jesus stops Martha and admonishes her to pause and focus on what's much more important– Jesus Himself. He reminds Martha that in her concentration on being busy she was missing out on life's centering moments. The problem was not that she was hardworking but that she was distracted.

I admit that I can identify with the busy and hard working Martha more than the contemplative Mary. In my worker mentality, I have been guilty of going through entire days with no pauses and no prayer time. In my nonstop productivity, I have given, as an offering, the things that I have "done" to support the work of the Lord instead of offering my complete attention in His presence.

Jesus lovingly warns Martha that there is something very wrong with this kind of thinking. One thing is needed, and that is to sit at the Lord's feet. When we get that right, our foundation is set for all of the other things to be fruitful. There is no foul in being busy but the level of priority must be granted to our Lord Jesus Christ.

Martha loved Jesus just as much as Mary. Yet, they were serving Him in two different ways. Martha served with her hands, and Mary served with her heart. It is the yielding of the heart that pleases God. With our culture's emphasis on resumes, personal brands, style, outputs, and performance, it is easy to begin to define ourselves by what we do. We have developed an intense focus on the "doing" much more than the "being." But, the works of our hands can become purposeless if they distract us from communing with God.

The very intent of my "To Do" list is to keep me focused and accountable to what needs to be done. However, when I find myself so entangled with the tasks of the hour, I remind myself that one thing is needed. The time that I spend with Jesus is more important than anything else. We may need to study stacks of pages, respond to a full inbox of emails and check off dozens of items on our task lists, but if Christ is not at the center, then all of it is for naught. It is merely a distraction of "To Do's".

The more completely we focus our attention on our Creator and Lord, the less chance there is of our being distracted…
Saint Ignatius

REJECTION AS A TOOL

Abraham got up early the next morning, got some food together and a canteen of water for Hagar, put them on her back and sent her away with the child. She wandered off into the desert of Beersheba. When the water was gone, she left the child under a shrub and went off, fifty yards or so. She said, "I can't watch my son die." As she sat, she broke into sobs. Meanwhile, God heard the boy crying. The angel of God called from Heaven to Hagar, "What's wrong, Hagar? Don't be afraid. God has heard the boy and knows the fix he's in. Up now; go get the boy. Hold him tight. I'm going to make of him a great nation."

Genesis 21:14-18, MSG

Rejection is a tool for divine placement and no story better emphasizes this idea than the story of Hagar, Abraham, and Sarah. Sarah and her husband Abraham grew impatient with the amount of time it was taking to conceive the child that God promised them. So, they took matters into their own hands and decided to have a child through Hagar, Sarah's maidservant. Hagar gave Abraham a son, Ishmael, but God later fulfilled His promise and Sarah gave birth to a son. As conflict brewed, Sarah asked Abraham to get rid of Hagar. Grievously, Abraham gave Hagar a bottle of water and a loaf of bread and sent her and her son away. This must have been an awful period of time for Hagar. She must have felt rejection in a deeply personal way. After all, she gave Abraham a child and was now being shown the door. However, the pain and sting of rejection is not without life lessons and three very powerful lessons can be learned in the rejection of Hagar.

First, rejection can bring about better placement. If I am in the wrong place, sometimes rejection is the only thing that can push me toward the right one. In this passage of scripture, rejection is used as a tool to send Hagar in the direction of her promise. We may ask God for a sports car and God may say, "No, take this bicycle. You need the exercise. You need to take your time in travel instead of speeding. Or maybe you need some humility for this journey." We don't always like the tools God chooses to get us to our destination but His plan always works in our favor.

Second, rejection is sometimes God's divinity superseding our flawed judgment. We will not always get what we want. What we want may hurt us. God protects us from things we really want but do not need. God's plans are greater than our most creative dreams. We may want God to give us Top Ramen because it's our favorite food when we're hungry but God won't do that if there is a five-course meal being prepared. We may need to be hungry for just a bit longer so that we can get what is ultimately much better for us.

Third, rejection can be a way of liberation. Hagar was sent away with her son Ishmael but she was released to her own place of promise. In the end, Hagar was so much better after having been freed from a situation she wasn't supposed to be in for the long haul. Rejection can liberate us so that we can climb upwards to our next level of life. God may dismiss something from your life today that would have distracted you or destroyed the path for your tomorrow.

Finally, we learn through Hagar's story that God is always faithful to His plan even in painful situations. She was not destroyed by rejection, but she went on to her new place in God.

No matter how painful rejection may feel, understand how powerful of a tool it can be. Rejection may be your blessing of this season to send you in the direction of your promise.

you

not wanting me

was

the beginning of me

wanting myself

thank you

Nayyirah Waheed

#TEAMNOSLEEP

The LORD is my shepherd, I lack nothing. He makes me lie down in green pastures, he leads me beside quiet waters, he refreshes my soul.

Psalm 23:1-3, NIV

In today's society many of us are more entrepreneurial, more independent, and more prone to wanting to do and have it all than ever before. It is rare to find someone focused on one occupation these days. Having a triple major in college is more prevalent and a surging amount of business executives own a "side" business. It is countercultural to talk about rest, meditation, and relaxation, or to take a true Sabbath when #TeamNoSleep is trending on Twitter. #TeamNoSleep became social media's popular way to say that someone is so committed to work that there is no time for sleep.

In college, I spent days without sleep trying to cram information before exams. In my adult life, I have stressed myself out over presentations and preparing for important meetings and events to the point of burnout. I have gone to the nearest coffee shop for that "blessing" of espresso in order to keep me awake longer than my body could handle. I was convinced that if I did not sacrifice sleep then the work wouldn't get done and I would miss out on an important opportunity. Where was my faith in those actions? How much do we trust God if we are committed to never resting? Do I really believe that God has the ability to bless the works of my hands if I choose to ignore God's commandment to rest my hands? It is a fine line indeed.

Like a computer, some of us need a system reboot. We are not even operating at our full capacity because there are too many windows open. We have not taken the time to allow ourselves to be refreshed or rejuvenated. We have a hard time with taking a Sabbath because we don't know how to make our well being a priority. In our minds, it is much more important to ensure that our children, friends, employees, partners, and projects have what they need before we can consider the needs of our own bodies.

I want you to remember that you are important to the work that you are doing along with the people that need you to live out your purpose. If there is never a time for you to recharge your body then you will be in a constant state of movement without focus. This is an unhealthy extreme. If too much of your belief lies in what you have to do, then you are operating in a capacity that leaves no room for God. I submit to you that rest takes faith.

God could have designed us in a way that omitted sleep as a requirement to survive but He designed rest as a part of our physical make up. We were made to rest because rest is an act of reliance on God. Rest is an act of faith. Furthermore, rest is an act of worship. How much are we worshipping God in the midst of our work? Our refusal to rest makes us servants of work and not servants of God. Proper rest says that I have done my part and God will honor both my work and my obedience.

Fear can keep you up all night, but faith makes one fine pillow.

Philip Gulley

LABEL-LESS... LIMITLESS... SYNONYMS

> Now when they saw the boldness of Peter and John, and perceived that they were uneducated, common men, they were astonished. And they recognized that they had been with Jesus.
>
> Acts 4:13, ESV

I am not the biggest fan of nametags at networking functions, but for the moment, this is a great illustration for how we often box others into labels. Never could you introduce all there is to really know about you within a 4x6 space that has room for only your name, and your professional association. But, how often do we assume that all there is to know about a person can be found within these confines?

There's something very discomforting about the ease in which we use labels not to *describe* but to *define*. There are all of these single labels that we affix to people. White. Minority. Single. Married. Poor. Educated. Dropout. Dark. Blonde. Gay. Liberal. Pro. Anti. I regularly find myself listening to polarizing debates that are solely based on the labels we place on others. How would our conversations change if we thought of people in a less limiting way? How do we judge or even dehumanize people by the labels we place on them? How do we limit God with the labels that we place on ourselves? Are we solely our profession? Our skin color? Our relationship status? Our age? Our political party?

Perceiving others within the confines of these labels is a slippery slope. God is leading us to suspend this inclination because it has the potential to justify limiting God and, very subtly, judging others. Let's not fall into the temptation of crucifying other people when they don't fit a limited definition of any one single characteristic.

We all walk this life in very different ways. We must be careful to be prayerful for others without imposing our own self-will and our own journey. Some people will have a difficult time with me preaching the Gospel and also enjoying a good happy hour, because it doesn't fit into their "Christian" label. Those who have a rigid picture of what healthy living looks like consider it strange that I am public about my love for exercise and clean eating but at a summer barbeque you will surely find me with a hot link and Purple Kool-Aid. Some may find discomfort listening to an urban youth, with tattoos, talk about salvation because it doesn't fit into their label of what it means to look holy. When we embrace this kind of categorization of others we put people in a box and take the seat of judgment that doesn't belong to us.

In Acts 4:13 we see the danger in underestimating people based solely on the limiting labels we place on them. Peter and John were looked upon with contempt because, as the Bible states, they were branded as uneducated men. But, there was something about them that made it difficult to confine them to that label. After they spent time with the Lord, they spoke with so much assurance and incredible knowledge, that men marveled at their boldness. Peter and John had exceeded the confines of their labels.

We are more than labels. Let us take the limits off of how we perceive others. Don't live with the perspective that identity can be boxed within any single definition. A balanced life is one with a limitless perspective. Having a personal relationship with Jesus should make a difference in your outlook and energize you to be label-less... limitless!

> *To insist on only these negative stories is to flatten my experience and to overlook the many other stories that formed me. The single story creates stereotypes. And the problem with stereotypes is not that they are untrue but that they are incomplete. They make one story become the only story... The consequence of the single story is this: it robs people of dignity. It makes our recognition of our equal humanity difficult. It emphasizes how we are different rather than how we are similar...*
>
> Chimimanda Adechi, Danger Of The Single Story

FORGIVING OUR FATHERS

Although my father and my mother have forsaken me, the Lord will take me up [adopt me as His child].

Psalm 27:10, AMP

One of the many striking realities of our generation is the overwhelming growth and effects of fatherlessness. The thread of fatherlessness is so weaved into the fabric of our generation that I read recently that 24 million people in America alone grow up in homes without their biological fathers and half of all children will be fatherless at some point during childhood. This substantiates taglines like the "Fatherless Generation."

I grew up without my father in the home, and for many years had a turbulent relationship with my mother. I related to Psalm 27:10 because I often searched for something to fill the void that existed. I would read this scripture passage so many times. I read it when the pain of separation impacted my relationship with others. I read it when I was angry at my absent father. I read it after intense arguments with my mother. I would read this passage and translate it to mean that God would take care of me, even if my parents could not. But as I have matured and embraced fully the concept of forgiveness and the understanding that we are all imperfect (including parents), it means something much deeper to me.

Now, I read this to mean that if my mother and father forsake me, the Lord will give me a greater patience and understanding for the imperfections of their humanity. That level of understanding can only be found in the Lord because it means to see them through the eyes that only God can give. This scripture illustrates that the Lord grants me His eyes when I need to see people in their frailty and mistakes and love them with a heart that sees through a grace-focused lens.

The Lord has taken me up. The Hebrew translation for this phrase is the Lord will gather me, that is, take me into his care and keeping. He will gather my emotions that make it so easy to judge fathers who have made the wrong decisions and mothers who have struggled to get it right. I love both of my parents. Regardless of any inadequacy I may have experienced, regardless of my father's absence growing up, regardless of my mother and I's continued inability to see eye to eye as mother-daughter in those teenage years, and regardless of my expectations for parents based on the family structure I grew up watching on The Cosby Show and at my friends' dinner tables. Regardless. The Lord has taken me up, and I understand how to love them as God loves me– unconditionally.

By God's grace and His protective power, I escaped many negative effects of fatherlessness but I still had many scars. Being "taken up" also provides a healing for these scars.

If 24 million American children live apart from their fathers, then what will it look like for that many adults to harbor unforgiveness, bitterness, and hate? Let us be elevated and moved to forgive our fathers. Let us be moved to forgive our parents as a whole for the sins of their own humanity. It can provide a healing balm for generations ahead.

Prayer:

My incredible Father, the only Father I know- thank You for taking me into your care. Teach me how to be a daughter that pleases You. Bless them who came together to give birth to me. You have called me to honor them. God, take me up. Grant me your eyes and your heart and help me to understand the wounds of my father and mother and love them through their wounds as you love me in spite of mine. Elevate me above my own inclination to judge and empower me to love completely.

Halleemah Nash, "Prayer For My Parents" Journal Entry

HOUSEBUILDING 101

Why do you call me, 'Lord, Lord,' and do not do what I say? As for everyone who comes to me and hears my words and puts them into practice, I will show you what they are like. They are like a man building a house, who dug down deep and laid the foundation on rock. When a flood came, the torrent struck that house but could not shake it, because it was well built. But the one who hears my words and does not put them into practice is like a man who built a house on the ground without a foundation. The moment the torrent struck that house, it collapsed and its destruction was complete.

Luke 6:46-49, NIV

The work of an architect, or a housebuilder– in the context of this passage, is something of an art form. The process of building a home takes planning, design, an understanding of the phases of construction, and a long list of details. Any architectural professional will tell you that the single most important first step in building a home is site preparation and foundation.

Luke 6:46-49 is Jesus' message to Christians on the importance of understanding this process. Jesus is preaching and in the conclusion of His sermon He gives this great illustration of someone approaching Him and calling Him Lord without having any real relationship. By using the parallels of two housebuilders, Jesus explains how dangerous that kind of interaction or lack thereof, can truly be.

One housebuilder builds his house on a firm foundation, and the other builds without a foundation in mind. The first housebuilder dug deep and built his house on a rock, taking time to prepare a stone foundation. That first builder must have known a little something about architectural planning, because in order to build a house effectively a foundation must be properly laid. The second builder may have wanted to save time or maybe just wasn't as knowledgeable of the importance of this step. Either way, this builder didn't really see the importance of a foundation because their house was built on ground. One translation says that it was built on sand.

What is so powerful about this parable is that it paints a picture of two contrasting frames of mind. The focus of this passage is not necessarily on the house but on the mind frame of the builder. Why did one house stand while the other saw destruction? The answer is simple– one housebuilder did what it took to lay a solid foundation while the other did not. The destruction was not a result of the storm. Storms are inevitable. The destruction was a result of negligence on the part of the housebuilder. The damage would not have been as bad had the second housebuilder only taken the time to build their house correctly.

The kind of foundation that we build our lives upon will determine whether we survive the storm or not. Until there is a serious commitment from us to get our foundation right, we will fall victim to destruction. Giving God ground-level Lordship over our lives is a house built on sand. God has no desire for a surface connection with us. God wants a deeply rooted relationship. This kind of relationship is the solid foundation that can withstand the strength of any raging storm.

The house of the wicked will be destroyed, but the tent of the upright will flourish.

Proverbs 14:11, NIV

STAY IN YOUR LANE

Surely God is good to Israel, to those who are pure in heart. But as for me, my feet had almost slipped; I had nearly lost my foothold. For I envied the arrogant, when I saw the prosperity of the wicked.

Psalm 73:1-3, NIV

I am an avid sports fan and in addition to NFL and NBA Playoffs, March Madness and The World Cup, the Summer Olympics is another one of those all consuming periods of time where life is enhanced through the glory of sport. USA sprinter Sanya Richards-Ross emerged as one of my favorite Olympians during the 2012 London Olympic Games. Her journey to triumph, which culminated in her first individual gold medal, was amazing to watch. For me, there was a critical preceding race that set the stage for this medal and made this such a beautiful victory. It was the race where she failed to reach the gold and took home the bronze four years earlier in the 2008 Beijing Olympic Games.

Going into the Women's 400-meter final in Beijing, Richards-Ross was the favorite to win the gold. She dominated and entered the home stretch with a commanding lead but then the unthinkable happened. British Olympian, Christine Ohuruogu gained the lead and Richards-Ross fell far behind, finishing third.

The race was replayed a few times in slow motion as the commentators tried to determine what happened. Richard-Ross stated that her hamstring began to bother her at 320 meters, and, of course Ohurougu ran an incredible race; but, there was something else that stuck out to me. There was a moment where you saw Richard-Ross' eyes peer over at her competitor Ohuruogu as she gained on her ultimately passing her to win. I thought about that moment when reading this passage.

How difficult it must be to run a race and see others gaining on you, running faster, and seemingly winning. How do you continue to run toward your goal without falling into the temptation of comparisons and allowing those comparisons to become distractions? Four words: stay in your lane.

I am learning to trust God despite what I often see around me. I have to look up and not to the right or the left because I can lose my confidence and my ability to master my own lane when I drift into someone else's. We can forget about the abundant blessings in our current space when we covet another one. We fall to the temptation of measuring our lives based on others' when we change our focus from God to our friends or even our foes. When our eyes are not set on the right thing, our feet can slip, as described in Psalm 73. The only way to sustain the kind of focus, patience, and endurance necessary for your win is to stay in your lane.

Sanya Richards-Ross was heartbroken after coming in third in Beijing, but she went on to win the gold medal in the London Olympic games. As tough as the Beijing loss was, there were lessons that I am sure that she learned. In an interview after her gold win, Richards-Ross credited the fact that she didn't shoot out or overextend herself. When she saw herself losing ground based on the position of the other runners, she paid attention. She paced herself, ran her best race and, in the end, she went home a champion.

If you come to a place where you're comparing yourself, the progression of your life, your career, or your spiritual journey to that of others– remember that there is a danger of losing your footing and losing sight of the race you should be running. If you simply complete the race that was designed for you to run, there is an amazing reward that awaits you.

I just been playing I aint even notice I was winning

Drake

FRONTIN'

When the ark of the Lord's covenant came into the camp, all Israel raised such a great shout that the ground shook. Hearing the uproar, the Philistines asked, "What's all the shouting in the Hebrew camp?" …So the Philistines fought, and the Israelites were defeated and every man fled to his tent. The slaughter was very great.

1 Samuel 4:5-6 and 10, NIV

Those of us who are under the age of 35 have been frequently called the Hip Hop Generation. A generation where our worldview is formed by the latest rap lyrics and role models are those seen on music videos and with the largest following on social media. Many say that this generation lives in a surface driven culture with a set of life goals that are lived without depth. In a hip hop summation of this assessment; we are often guilty of frontin'.

In the urban dictionary, frontin' is defined in this way:

> to put up a facade or make appearances, typically to impress or in some way deceive to maintain image.

The Israelites were accused of the same blunder, and in this story we see the how hazardous the consequences can be. The Israelites and Philistines, who were archenemies, were at war. The first battle ended in Israel's defeat and the Israelites got a little uneasy. After this defeat they decided to take a different approach and bring the Ark of the Covenant into their camp. The Ark of the Covenant symbolized God's presence. Their hope was that this symbol would save them from the hand of their enemies.

It is important to note that the Philistines feared the God of the Israelites. The Philistines remembered stories about God's intervention for Israel when they left Egypt. They were familiar with the plagues, the parting of the Red Sea, and the Israelites' release from captivity. Nevertheless, when it came down to it, the Philistines did not see a good enough reason to back down from battle. To them, all Israel possessed was a *symbol* of victory. Frontin' was not enough. They faced off in a second battle and the Israelites suffered a great defeat.

We front too. We want the appearance of holiness, virtue, strength and power, but below the surface there is nothing really there. We attend churches where the Word of God is rightly divided but when it comes time for application we hide the Word in our hearts but do not allow it to have life. We put on the whole armor of God– the belt of truth, breastplate of righteousness, shield of faith, helmet of salvation, and sword of the Spirit. But, when faced with battle we cower– not truly understanding that victory is sure if we just use what we have.

The Israelites thought that the Ark of the Covenant would protect them. They were using God like a good luck charm. They looked to a symbol to guide them instead of the real thing. And in the end, they lost. What a brilliant way to portray the results of lack of authenticity.

Just like an oasis will not quench your thirst in the desert and lip-synching will not win at American Idol, a *symbol* of faith will not give you the victory when it's time for battle! The question we must ask ourselves is are we grounded by faith in the One who can transform, change, renew, and deliver? Or, are we clinging to a symbol that creates an appearance of valor and virtue. Do I believe? Or, am I just frontin'?

The authentic self is soul made visible

Sarah Ban Breathnach

GET FOCUSED

About three o'clock in the morning Jesus came to them, walking on the water. When the disciples saw him, they screamed in terror, thinking he was a ghost. But Jesus spoke to them at once. "It's all right," he said. "I am here! Don't be afraid." Then Peter called to him, "Lord, if it's really you, tell me to come to you by walking on water." "All right, come," Jesus said. So Peter went over the side of the boat and walked on the water toward Jesus. But when he looked around at the high waves, he was terrified and began to sink. "Save me, Lord!" he shouted. Instantly Jesus reached out his hand and grabbed him. "You don't have much faith," Jesus said. "Why did you doubt me?" And when they climbed back into the boat, the wind stopped. Then the disciples worshiped him. "You really are the Son of God!" they exclaimed.

Matthew 14:25-33, NLT

This is that familiar story of a very bold Peter with the disciples out on a boat in the Sea of Galilee. After Jesus finished praying, He saw that His disciples were in a raging storm. So, He went out to them, walking on water. Peter saw this and said, "Lord if it's really you, bid me to come to you on the water." The Lord did just that, but the condition was that Peter would have to focus and keep his eyes on Jesus. Peter got out of the boat and walked on the water, but the moment he took his eyes off the Lord and focused on the storm he started to sink.

When we lose focus and take our eyes off of Jesus, it's easy to drown. We drown in our circumstances, in the gravity of our storms, and in the responsibilities that consume our days. We can become concerned with the wrong things and lose focus when we take our eyes off Him. Where's the focus of your faith?

I encourage you to spend a period of time just finding focus. Regroup and center your gaze on Christ. This is important because God has plans beyond your current placement and a future beyond your present but getting you there will require a direct focus on the Lord. This whole business of walking on water sounds so strange, but what has God spoken into your life that seems equally impossible? What seems out of range, or difficult to make real in your mind? God says, "Come. Walk towards it. Walk towards what seems too distant and have faith that nothing is impossible with Me."

I heard in a sermon that "challenges hang out in the general vicinity of what's possible." If we just direct our attention on Jesus we won't need to be rescued from the winds and the rain. We can operate with power in the midst of trouble and we can do the miraculous by faith. Like Jesus, we can walk on water in the face of the storm, if we can just focus our intention on Him.

Prayer:

Father, grant us renewed focus. Grant us a renewed faith. Restore unto us the joy of our salvation and give us the energy we need to get back in the race if we've been sidelined. Help us eliminate things that look good and seem important but only cause us to forget You. Help us to focus on the main thing. Bring our lives, our agendas, or plans into submission of Your will and Your way. Set our gaze away from our circumstances. Keep us from drowning. Father we trust you beyond our circumstance. We believe beyond what we can see. Help us to finish strong by finishing with focus on You.

Halleemah Nash, Midweek Prayer Call

CONQUERING KING

Create in me a pure heart, O God, and renew a steadfast spirit within me. Do not cast me from your presence or take your Holy Spirit from me. Restore to me the joy of your salvation and grant me a willing spirit, to sustain me. Then I will teach transgressors your ways, so that sinners will turn back to you. Deliver me from the guilt of bloodshed, O God, you who are God my Savior, and my tongue will sing of your righteousness. Open my lips, Lord, and my mouth will declare your praise. You do not delight in sacrifice, or I would bring it; you do not take pleasure in burnt offerings. My sacrifice, O God, is a broken spirit; a broken and contrite heart you, God, will not despise.

Psalm 51:10-17, NIV

One of my favorite worship songs is "Jesus You Are My Life." It is a song confessing the desire to be totally consumed by God. Admittedly, there have been times in my relationship with God where I've acted more like a spoiled child wanting my own way than a mature woman of faith. I have even taken matters into my own hands when I grew impatient with God's timing. I have turned from God and found myself on the carousel of consequences that resulted from my bad decisions and lack of obedience. The hard lesson I learned was that one unregretted sin could lead to another and spiral out of control. In these instances, it was easy to fall deeper into sin and feel separated from God. This path always leads to brokenness.

David was familiar with this path and in Psalm 51 he hit his own brick wall and found himself broken by his own doing. Although David was remembered as a man after God's heart, his own heart had to be conquered first. This extraordinary Psalm was David's prayer of confession and his prayer for forgiveness. He prayed that God would rescue him from himself and gift him with more of God's spirit and less of his own. In this passage, David is a repentant sinner that is ready to give up his own way. David was before God, bare and broken with all of the weaknesses of his own will. To review, David committed adultery with another man's wife, he tried to cover up her pregnancy, and had her husband murdered. Yet, in his brokenness, David stood in Psalm 51 as a fortress ready and willing to be conquered.

God can do such amazing things in broken spaces. I learned God-worship when my pride was shattered. Have you ever been completely torn down by the mess that you made in your own life? Has conviction ever overcome you to the point of tears? When I find myself in this place I return to this Psalm and I sing that favorite song of mine:

> "O' conquering King, conquer my heart,
> and make of me a pleasing gift to God.
> My love for you will never die.
> Jesus, You are my life."

Being dead set in my own way has never built much of anything, but it has certainly destroyed a few things. I am grateful for the many occasions when God blessed me by conquering me and bringing down the mountain of my own way.

It is not the mountain we conquer, but ourselves…

Edmund Hillary, First Man To Climb Mt Everest

DON'T BE A HATER

For wherever there is jealousy and selfish ambition, there you will find disorder and evil of every kind.

James 3:16, NLT

I have always considered jealousy an unusual emotion. This verse in James 3, points to how poisonous jealousy has the potential to be. Jealousy never stops as a singular emotion. It is a tool that Satan uses to strategically deprive us of our own self-confidence, our gratefulness, and sometimes to sever important relationships.

A while back, one of my very best friends invited me over for some girlfriend time. As was our tradition, we enjoyed dinner and some television and caught up on what was happening at work. At the end of the evening she asked if she could share something personal with me. It seemed like a silly question since we shared just about everything. However, the look on her face told me that this would be something new. We had recently worked on a project together and she admitted intentionally distancing herself because she felt that she was doing so much work and I was receiving most of the acknowledgement. She found herself trying to make sense of her own anger until she realized that the anger she felt had become a form of jealousy.

I remember being blown away for a number of reasons. For one, she was someone that I'd greatly looked up to. And two, this was shocking because it shined a light on how easily jealousy can creep into relationships and everyday circumstances. How was it possible that my friend, someone I considered a peer-mentor, could feel jealousy towards me? Had I also experienced this same thing with other friendships? Had I ever distanced myself from a girlfriend because I secretly wanted to be where she was or resented her for something she had that I did not?

There, in the standing mirror, was that ugly dress women wear called envy. Make no mistake, men envy too. But from my personal experience, when it rears it's head amongst women it leads the way for destructive thoughts that can choke the life out of sisterly relationships. Where there is envy there is also room for deceit. And in the case of my girlfriend, I did not want to open the door to any of these vices.

I honored my friend for being so honest about something that must have been difficult to admit. I didn't judge her for her feelings. Instead, I asked my friend if she wouldn't mind kneeling with me to pray. I wanted to kneel together to outwardly symbolize our equal need for God's strength in our lives and our mutual fallen condition. That night I prayed with my friend. I thanked God for her honesty and asked God to relieve her of any guilt, and to forgive her of her envy. I also asked God to help me to overcome my own jealousy towards other friends I'd compared myself to. It was a great moment for us.

James 3:16 speaks to jealousy's active potential to become much more destructive. So, we have to cut it off at the head. Ten years later, the woman that I am speaking of is still one of my best friends who has taught me so much about God's love. If you find yourself hating or envying your neighbor, submit yourself to prayer. Jealousy and envy are often the devil's ways of separating you from someone who can shepherd you through both the hills and valleys of life. Don't be stripped of that. Don't be a hater.

Jealousy is a sickness…
Savon in "Love Jones"

THE HOPE DEALER

For I know the plans I have for you," declares the LORD "plans to prosper you and not to harm you, plans to give you hope and a future.

Jeremiah 29:11-14, NIV

Growing up in the inner city during the crack epidemic of the 1980s, I had a front row view of the social ills that resulted from widespread drug addiction. As an adolescent it was difficult to wrap my mind around it. I couldn't see all of the layers underneath the first introduction to a drug that made addiction so welcoming. In hindsight, what I saw as a preteen in my old neighborhood in California now makes sense with my spiritual eyes.

I saw drug dealers hanging around despair, destruction and emotional instability. For a person who cannot see the promise beyond their current pain, there is something appealing about a temporary high. This picture is very similar to what was happening in the community that was being addressed in Jeremiah 29. This is Jeremiah's letter to a group of people who were disheartened and in disrepair during a really troubling time in Israel's history. After being exiled from their place of comfort, this was a population of people who had a hope deficiency, and God directed Jeremiah to speak words of encouragement to them in the midst of that season.

This is not an unfamiliar place for many of us. Have you ever found yourself in certain situations where you were once hopeful and optimistic, but have since lost hope? Although this is a common challenge, it is also a precarious and vulnerable place. This place is Satan's play zone because when we are discouraged it is easier to give up. It is easier to yield to accepting fear, self-pity, and disbelief. It is also easy to become addicted to what is destructive to us. Satan's whispers in these seasons are debilitating.

The enemy inserts himself into this destructive space like the dealer who offers that temporary high, and that false hope at a moment of vulnerability. Jeremiah 29 is our scriptural reminder that God understands where we *are* but wants us to understand what He *knows*. God knows that there is an incredible plan and like the exiles Jeremiah is addressing in this passage, we often cannot see it because of what we are going through. Nevertheless, there is a plan to give us a hope and a future. Remember that God thinks about us personally so this is a personal plea. God is saying, "I know the plans I have for you."

You may not be spared pain, drama, or hardship, but God is going to see you through to an amazing conclusion. I encourage you to put hope in your permanent windshield. That means that you can be excited about what you hope for. Be patient in the midst of what's uncomfortable, and commit yourself to prayer while the thing that you hope for is on the way. If you've lost your hope, know that you don't need a temporary high that leads to destruction. Like the Israelites in Jeremiah 29, you need the Hope Dealer. God wants to restore your hope today and remind you that all is not lost. Regardless of what it looks like, there is a plan for you— a plan that will give you a future and a hope.

O Lord, in whom is our hope, remove far from us, we pray Thee, empty hopes and presumptuous confidence. Make our hearts so right with Thy most holy and loving heart, that hoping in Thee we may do good; until that day when faith and hope shall be abolished by sight and possession, and love shall be all in all.

Anonymous

PRAYER

Devote yourselves to prayer, keeping alert in it with an attitude of thanksgiving.

Colossians 4:2, NAS

Although modern technology has created such amazing advances in our lives, it has also destroyed our ability to communicate in many instances. If technology is not leveraged adequately, technological advances can be barriers for effective communication and relationship management. Virtual conversations have become instinctual. Verbal conversations, heartfelt letters, and a clear ability to communicate with sincerity are all becoming a rarity. I have communicated virtually with people for months before ever having a real conversation. I also catch myself speaking in acronyms, short hand, and 140 characters. For the sake of time and convenience, I send mass text messages and engage over email instead of engaging individuals. Sometimes I even "post" on social media before I pray.

More than a tool for convenience, technology has also become a scapegoat used to release us from confrontations and difficult conversations. Nevertheless, it is not a substitution for prayer. Prayer requires personal interaction. It is our vehicle for communication and the only search engine that leads to God. Through prayer we experience relationship and intimacy with

God. Consequentially, the quality of our prayer life determines the quality of our relationship.

The same way that new age forms of communication cannot replace the sound of a loved one's voice saying "I love you," nothing can replace prayer. Minister and teacher Oswald Chambers said, "Prayer does not fit us for the greater work; prayer is the greater work." Although technology is a wonderful tool that can assist us in developing and strengthening our prayer lives, prayer itself is irreplaceable.

The challenge, in the evolving world of communication, is to keep our prayers sincere before God. Don't think of prayer the same way that you think of Facebook posts. Don't fall into our cultural norm of making communication a consistent surface proclamation. Don't think of prayer the same way that you think of retweets and regrams. Don't make prayer a lengthy monologue with words from someone else's communication with God. Let prayer be communication to God from your own heart.

If praying feels intimidating to you, that's okay. Recite the Lord's Prayer daily and let that be the starting point in your goal of devoting yourself to prayer. What does that look like, you ask? One practical exercise is to make quick brief prayers your response to every situation throughout your day. I like to write post-it notes with Psalms in various places to remind myself of prayers that I need to speak aloud. You don't have to isolate yourself from other people and your daily work in order to pray constantly. I have friends that do, but it is not a requirement. Engage in intentional activities to strengthen your prayer life. Don't let technology be a barrier, let it be a building block for a greater prayer life.

Through prayer I become one in love with Christ. I realize that praying to Him is loving Him.

Mother Teresa

THE PITY PARTY DOES NOT TURN UP

> Death and life are in the power of the tongue, and those who love it will eat its fruits.
>
> Proverbs 18:21, NKJV

The tongue can be used as a poison or medicine. We are walking through life with this powerful weapon right underneath our noses. Its power is so great that, depending on how it's used, it is capable of producing life or death. The Bible tells us that our words are so powerful that they can bless or curse, encourage or discourage, hurt or heal, tear down or build up. Our words can influence the way we act and feel as well as determine our attitude and outlook on life.

Have you ever said to your friends, before you went out to a function, "I don't know why we are going, it will likely be uneventful, I am sure this will just be a waste of a nice outfit." Then, when you get there, you commence to say, "See. I knew I shouldn't have come. This was a waste of a nice outfit." Conversely, when you make the conscious decision to say, "It doesn't matter who is there and what happens, I am getting ready to have the time of my life" – generally the evening follows suit.

Self-pity works in the same way. Understand that words have power. How careful are you about what you say especially when you are in the midst of a challenge? Have you ever talked yourself out of your purpose? Or, took yourself out of the game before it started? Have you found yourself saying things like, "No one understands. This will never get better. Everyone is in a better place than I am...." If so, you are having a pity party and there is nothing fun about it.

Avoiding the pity party scene is the simplest principle, yet one of the most difficult areas in our lives to discipline. No wonder the enemy tries to bombard our minds with evil thoughts of doubt, fear, and discouragement. The pity party is the enemy's tool to keep our minds bound. And some of us fall for it every time. The Bible says in 2 Corinthians 10:5 that we are to "cast down imaginations, and every high thing that exalteth itself against the knowledge of God, and bring into captivity every thought to the obedience of Christ."

Your speech has active power that can change both outlook and circumstance. Jesus did not instruct us to talk *about* the mountain but rather talk *to* the mountain. Faith will move mountains when and only when it is released with the words of your mouth. How you view your circumstances is all about what you speak.

If the enemy can get you to the place where you will say what you feel, rather than saying what God says- he has got you. You may as well pull out the streamers and let the pity party begin. Being in a discouraged place can be consuming but with the help of the Holy Spirit, we can be saved from the destructive power of our own words. We can purposely order our conversation and speak carefully chosen words of God that will not only produce victory in our own life but in the lives of others. Don't be a Debby Downer. Debby Downers are people that constantly dwell on hardships whether real or imagined. Regardless of what we face, we have joy in the Lord and are blessed beyond measure. When you find yourself wrestling with feelings of self-pity, remind yourself that you have death and life right there in your tongue. So, which one will you choose to speak?

Start calling yourself healed, happy, whole, blessed, and prosperous. Stop talking to God about how big the mountains are and start talking to your mountains about how big your God is!

Joel Osteen

SLINGSHOT PRACTICE...ON THE HILLTOP

David answered, "You come at me with sword and spear and battle-ax. I come at you in the name of God-of-the-Angel-Armies, the God of Israel's troops, whom you curse and mock. This very day God is handing you over to me. I'm about to kill you, cut off your head, and serve up your body and the bodies of your Philistine buddies to the crows and coyotes. The whole earth will know that there's an extraordinary God in Israel. And everyone gathered here will learn that God doesn't save by means of sword or spear. The battle belongs to God - he's handing you to us on a platter!" That roused the Philistine, and he started toward David. David took off from the front line, running toward the Philistine. David reached into his pocket for a stone, slung it, and hit the Philistine hard in the forehead, embedding the stone deeply. The Philistine crashed, facedown in the dirt. That's how David beat the Philistine– with a sling and a stone.

1 Samuel 17:45-50, MSG

Everyone has goals that in certain occasions can seem unreachable. For me, it was the process of applying to college. Like many first generation college students, I didn't know much about the college process. I didn't have a network of people in my direct circle who attended college, let alone graduated from one. Higher education, for me, was a giant. 1 Samuel was my mirror and motivation for what God makes possible in the face of unreachable goals.

This passage illustrates how David not only slayed Goliath but later on achieved greatness because he believed that God was bigger than any giant he faced. David, a lowly shepherd boy who was overlooked by his family and peers, went on to become a king and do great things despite what he may have lacked.

Despite poor standardized test scores, a lackluster academic record, and the fact that I resided in a city with the highest homicide rate in the state at the time, in the fall of 1998 I was accepted to Howard University and traveled to Washington, DC as an incoming freshman. It is so fitting that Howard is built on the highest plain in the nation's capital, affectionately called "The Hilltop." As a freshman, I had many Goliaths to slay– figuring out tuition with little money and minimal support, being bold in spite of modest confidence, keeping pace academically after performing poorly on entry exams for college level Math and English and having to take remedial courses to catch up, and overcoming low self-esteem in a world of gorgeous women who seemed to have it all.

In the beginning, all of these giants seemed unconquerable. Nevertheless, I perfected my slingshot strategy. I built my confidence by studying God's Word, I wore my armor, I answered fear with faith, I walked in God's favor, and I put my trust in His power to grant me victory despite what I faced. I became skilled in slaying Goliaths for four straight years until I mounted the Hilltop as a graduate.

I felt like David– chosen by God to become a testimony of what God can do with yielded vessels from meek beginnings. David became a King, and I became a Howard University graduate. Attending Howard University meant more to me than any accomplishment or specific experience. Being granted the opportunity to obtain a higher education leveled the playing field and introduced me to a network and a world that I could have never imagined at one time. My acceptance to Howard gifted me with challenges to overcome and I thank God for every one of them. I encourage you to remember David as you face your own giants with faith that your victory is sure regardless of where you begin.

Your beginnings will seem humble, so prosperous will your future be.

Job 8:7, NIV

PRAYERS FOR OUR EXES

You're familiar with the old written law, 'Love your friend,' and its unwritten companion, 'Hate your enemy.' I'm challenging that. I'm telling you to love your enemies. Let them bring out the best in you, not the worst. When someone gives you a hard time, respond with the energies of prayer, for then you are working out of your true selves, your God-created selves. This is what God does. He gives his best—the sun to warm and the rain to nourish—to everyone, regardless.

Matthew 5:43-46, MSG

For many, the most contentious relationship we have is with our ex partner. We have a tendency to villainize our exes in a way that only threatens our personal growth. Matthew 5 gives us a prescription for healing in this area.

I went through the toughest breakup of my life not long ago and it was difficult to think about my ex boyfriend, or the relationship, partly because it ended in such devastating heartbreak. After a two and a half year romance I felt I was left with only tears, questions, and a newly developed insecurity. Although it wasn't God's will that we would last forever, I became consumed with painful parts of the relationship, which clouded a wonderful season of love and lessons. At the time, I couldn't bear to think of him or even share the same space. I remember reading this verse in Matthew 5 in the midst of a wave of emotions that I was feeling. It was at this moment that

God led me to pray for my ex boyfriend every day for seven consecutive days. I would pray for his family, his career, and I would even pray for the woman that he would one day call his wife. As you can imagine, this was one of the hardest things I have ever done. It was heart wrenching. But it was also cathartic. With every prayer I felt a weight lifted. I felt a release. I was beginning to experience what it felt like to truly forgive him.

With time, I could clearly see that my ex was no demon just as I was no saint. We'd both made costly mistakes that hurt one another. But, in praying for him despite my emotions I discovered the essence of this message– forgiveness is about our own freedom. Forgiveness is for you. It has nothing to do with whether or not the people who hurt you really deserve it. If we are honest, none of us deserved the gift God gave us in Christ or the price Christ paid on the cross so that we could be forgiven. This truth is so eloquently stated in Matthew 5, "This is what God does. He gives his best…regardless." In our quest to mirror His image, this is our challenge.

Understand that the release you crave from certain relationships and experiences can only be found when you fully forgive. Forgiveness doesn't only mean to pardon someone else. It means to let go. Sometimes a lack of forgiveness is an anvil. Unforgiveness weighs us down and prevents us from moving forward. Here's the test: if you are at a grocery store or at church, or at a party two stepping– and your ex walks in and you feel like you just had a stroke, then you have work to do.

Today, I could run into an ex, regardless of how it ended, and see God's providence. In the case of the ex that I spent time in prayer for, I could see God's hand above our flaws and how God used our separation to make him a better man and me a better woman. This was no easy thing. It was an emotional triathlon of a process. But the act of prayer on behalf of someone that I held so much contempt for was therapeutic. I am no longer weighed down and have no anvil anchoring me in a bitter and painful place. Forgiveness granted me freedom. How many of you have ever prayed for your ex? I submit to you this truth– unless you can pray fervently for your ex, without experiencing physical pain, discomfort, bitterness and nausea, then you have not truly forgiven and let go. Pray for them until you do. It will free you.

We must develop and maintain the capacity to forgive. He who is devoid of the power to forgive is devoid of the power to love. There is some good in the worst of us and some evil in the best of us. When we discover this, we are less prone to hate our enemies.

Dr. Martin Luther King Jr.

FEARLESS YOU...

Don't be afraid, because I am with you. Don't be intimidated; I am your God. I will strengthen you. I will help you. I will support you with my victorious right hand.

Isaiah 41:10, GWT

Last summer I was working with youth at a summer park district program. I remember feeling particularly enlightened during the time spent in the pool area observing the difference in how children and adults approached swimming instruction. Watching how individuals handled swimming was like being in a classroom learning a great lesson on fear. Adults approached the water slowly and carefully. They talked through all the reasons why they didn't like water and why they couldn't swim. The children, however, approached swimming with a sense of adventure. They jumped, dove, caught on to the principles of swimming quickly, and had an altogether blast. Children faced the water in a way that seemed brave in comparison to the adults.

Some lessons taught in the water can be translated into real life. What makes children so courageous is something that can be learned by many adults. Children play in the present moment. They have no anxiety about failure or injury or outside perception. The difference between the children and the adults was– fear. Adults seemingly allow the fear of failure and what we cannot control to become a very present obstacle.

When we worry too much about what others think or the outcome of our decisions we are not "playing" in the present moment. We become too afraid of the unknown. We are too nervous about failing. We are scared to make mistakes or to be embarrassed and this hinders us from just "going for it."

Fear is not a spirit that we were given for our progress but it is a spirit that we must overcome in order to see our progress! In 2 Timothy 1:7 Paul says, "For God hath not given us the spirit of fear; but of power, and of love, and of a sound mind."

Deep seated fear is an agent of paralysis. Fear keeps us safe, but it also prevents us from moving forward. There is such hope and promise in the future if we can just overcome fear. Fear of the unknown can be a stumbling block. But, hope, and the understanding that we are protected by the God who will never leave us and will uphold us in the water, is our salvation from fear.

If we really believe that God is with us and we are never forsaken then what do we have to fear? Be fearless! Everything that we need to overcome what we fear is granted to us in God.

What would you accomplish and step forward into if you weren't afraid? If you weren't bound by what people may think or whether or not you would be accepted – what decisions would you make? What does a fearless you look like?

Don't fear. Dive into the water. Swim as if failure was a nonexistent term. Swim good.

"Fear can hold you prisoner, hope can set you free"
Andy in "Shawshank Redemption"

WINERY REVELATIONS

"My Father is the vinedresser…"

John 15:1, AMP

As a newly self-proclaimed oenophile, I recently took a trip to Napa Valley for a tour of three historic wineries. I had hoped to enhance my knowledge of the region's best wine selections but was particularly fascinated with the journey of the grapes. I wondered how the grapes transformed to become what is considered a premium palatal experience. The answer became simple as the tour progressed: it is all about the vine process.

The job description of the vinedresser is to care for and prune the vine for maximum results. Responsibilities include weekly observation of the health of the grapes, pest and disease monitoring, crop estimations, and overall care and cultivation. The vinedresser commits to understanding all there is to know about the needs of the vine including the necessary pressure the vines must endure to produce savory grapes.

All in all, vinedressing is all about stress. Water stress to be exact. Water stress is a physiological state that grapevines experience when there is insufficient water supply. Like any livestock, when the vine thinks it's dying then there is a frantic energy and high-level reproduction that follows. Vinedressers often use the phrases "making them suffer" and "stressing them out" when referring to the process used to get the absolute best out of the grapes. The vine produces at a high level when it has endured heat and stress from the vinedresser. In other words, in order to achieve maximum production– there has to be intense stress, but just the right amount, according to the expertise of the vinedresser.

Grapes have no idea what the ultimate purpose of this stressful process will be. They haven't been made privy to the fact that they are being stressed so that they can one day become a delightful wine. They are just stressed out grapes thinking that this is all that there is. But the vinedresser knows that there is more to the story than the stress they are enduring. The vinedresser can look at the grape and see its future identity. Vinedressers see the necessity of this process in connection to the grapes' purpose. What a beautiful arrow pointed to God's care for us.

John 15 draws a parallel between God and this very personal connective process. Jesus says, "My Father is the vinedresser." Just as the vinedresser cares for the vine, God knows, cares for, and is knowledgeable of the development of Christians. God can see the stresses of life that often weigh us down. God can also see every single thing that will be necessary for us to fulfill our purpose. Who we are will be tested both by external forces, situations, trials, and often times every day haters. But who we are to become is also found, strengthened, and developed by God through stress. The vinedressing process is a long commitment before those grapes become what we see in those beautiful wine bottles. In the same way, God is committed to our development.

Greatness is in store when we are the best versions of ourselves. Becoming our best is sometimes attained after we too have been stressed out and made to suffer for a season.

Our Father is our vinedresser. He is the guarantee for our growth and fruitfulness. In the midst of the most stressful situations remember that we are still cared for and loved by God.

A diamond is just a piece of coal that handled stress exceptionally well.

Unknown

REPLAY

When my soul is in the dumps, I rehearse everything I know of you…Chaos calls to chaos, to the tune of whitewater rapids. Your breaking surf, your thundering breakers crash and crush me. Then God promises to love me all day, sing songs all through the night! My life is God's prayer.

Psalm 42:6-8, MSG

I read this scripture passage on New Year's Eve as I prepared for an exciting transition from one year to the next. With the New Year comes a certain natural vivacity. We create resolutions, the gym is always crowded with those determined to get fit, and social media is flooded with "new year new me" slogans. However, after about two or three months into the year all of this reverts back to a routine of allowing challenges to steal the motivation that we are ceremoniously granted with new seasons.

When you find yourself so easily robbed of that new season vigor I encourage you to read this passage. In Psalm 42, David is saying, "I need to rehearse in the theatre of my mind all that God has done when what I see and how I feel causes me to be consumed with negativity." If we are not careful, selective amnesia can set in alongside life's ups and downs. When this happens, our challenges become bigger than the abundant blessings that God has so consistently given us minute by minute. David had to remind himself that, in these moments, the best strategy is to revive our perspective. We have to focus on all that we know of God's love and ability. We may need to ask God to bring us into remembrance of His grace, mercy, loving-kindness, and His ability to make the impossible a very present reality.

Remaining in a grateful place takes effort. Be like David and rehearse everything you know to be true about God. When you start stepping out of all the things that God has spoken to you in this season of newness, and when life knocks you on your behind and makes you unsure of yourself– travel in your memory to the places where God has done His greatest work in your life. Rehearse in your memory when God made a way even when it seemed there was zero possibility. Remember when God healed you and provided a way of escape. Remember those blessings that so easily become overshadowed when Satan reminds you of who and what you are not. Bring back to your memory the times when God blessed you out of lack although you didn't deserve what you were given. Remember when God put you in the front when your effort should have kept you in the back. Remember the joy of your salvation. Rehearse in your mind how God resurrected dead situations in your life. Remember who God is and what God has done. Put the blessings of the Lord on replay.

"When you struggle with trust, go back to the curb on college move-in day when you didn't have enough money and no clue how you were going to stay in Washington, DC and you were able to move into the dorm anyway. That's God showing up. When you couldn't make ends meet and the next year you were in Europe. That's God showing up. When God closed professional doors you thought were yours and you ended up getting the job you always wanted in sports philanthropy. That's God showing up. Everything that you couldn't imagine then has manifested itself. Because God has not forgotten. Replay this record. It bangs."

Halleemah Nash, Prayer Journal

YOUR DESIGN IS ON PURPOSE

The word of the LORD came to me, saying, "Before I formed you in the womb I knew you, before you were born I set you apart; I appointed you as a prophet to the nations." "Alas, Sovereign LORD," I said, "I do not know how to speak; I am too young." But the LORD said to me, "Do not say, 'I am too young.' You must go to everyone I send you to and say whatever I command you. Do not be afraid of them, for I am with you and will rescue you," declares the LORD. Then the LORD reached out his hand and touched my mouth and said to me, "I have put my words in your mouth. See, today I appoint you over nations and kingdoms to uproot and tear down, to destroy and overthrow, to build and to plant.

Jeremiah 1:4-10, NIV

It's remarkable how intricately designed we are. Even with what we are insecure about, we are still designed intentionally. It doesn't matter what you don't have and what mistakes you've made. God designed you! Stop pointing out your inadequacies and instead say, "I am beautiful and amazing and I love what God has designed." Your inabilities, your frailties, and even the shortcomings that give you the most pain, are on purpose.

This reminds me of the story of one of my favorite heroines Celestine Tate. Tate was born with arthrogryposis multiplex, a condition that erodes connective tissue. In her case, it greatly reduced her limb development and left her quadriplegic. Her parents deserted her early on and she was raised by her grandparents. Tate was very smart and finished high school in 3 years. She wasn't able to walk but she could crawl using her arms and legs. In spite of her condition, she became a mother and gave birth to a daughter. When the courts attempted to take her child, claiming that she was unfit to raiser her, Tate shocked the courtroom by changing her daughter's diaper using only her teeth, and kept custodial rights. She went on to take music lessons and even became a working musician. Tate, who didn't have the capacity of her limbs, became a mother and an accomplished musician. The question I asked myself after learning about Tate's story was— what am I doing with all the capacity of my limbs, my mind, and my body?

Celestine Tate is an example of the ultimate maximization of what God has given and living a full life. You will never have enough money, you will never have enough time, and you will never have it all together. But, go forth with God's design for your life. With all that you have and all that you do not have, the Lord has built you on purpose.

Do not waste your time with making excuses! In the first chapter of Jeremiah, God tells him that his excuses are no longer worthy of God's time. Spend your time focusing on the effort it will take to push beyond what you feel. This is a much better use of your time. Remembering to keep mind over matter will help you overcome your temptation to make excuses.

Excuses are merely illusions that you convince yourself are real so that you can accept being basic. Who you are and what you can become is everything but that.

Lift up the prayer in Jeremiah 32:17, "Ah, Sovereign LORD, you have made the heavens and the earth by your great power and outstretched arm. Nothing is too hard for you." Jeremiah offered up his inadequacies and God returned to him a great future to posses. Don't give God excuses. Push through and give God your greatness. It's in your design.

To accept ourselves as we are is to value our imperfections as much as our perfections.

Sandra Bierig

DISRUPTION OF THE STATISTICS

While Jesus was still speaking, someone came from the house of Jairus, the synagogue leader. "Your daughter is dead," he said. "Don't bother the teacher anymore." Hearing this, Jesus said to Jairus, "Don't be afraid; just believe, and she will be healed." When he arrived at the house of Jairus, he did not let anyone go in with him except Peter, John and James, and the child's father and mother. Meanwhile, all the people were wailing and mourning for her. "Stop wailing," Jesus said. "She is not dead but asleep."

Luke 8:49-52, NIV

In 2013, I watched the documentary *Dark Girls* with a few friends. It was a controversial analysis of colorism and the prejudices that women with dark skin face, particularly in American society. The statistics incorporated in the film were maddening. According to *Dark Girls*, most young black girls have a poor self-image, black women have a much lower chance at marriage, and "41.9 percent of black women in America have never been married in comparison to 20.7 percent of white women have never been married." These statistics don't paint much of a hopeful portrait for "dark girls" to look forward to. This portrayal was especially hard for me to swallow. As a single African-American woman with dark skin, I saw myself specifically in the film. This documentary wasn't just about the women featured, it was about me!

In my devotion time the very next morning I was led to this passage. It was the perfect moment to read about Jesus' interaction with Jairus and be reminded of how God interfaces with these kinds of alarming numbers. Jesus comes to disrupt the statistics. The Lord will disrupt the sensible, the rational, and the logical, which we often rely on as the ultimate truth. In this passage, we see the Lord showing us that He has the power to override the statistics and the ability to give life to dead situations. What looks absolutely dead to you? What looks impossible in your life right now? What looks like it is just not going to happen?

Jesus asks that we give Him a chance to beat the odds! Although it seems dead, it is not dead! It may look that way but there can be life if we just have faith. There are some amazing things that may look dead but are only lying dormant, and what unlocks their ability to live is our faith!

Fill in the blanks here: Statistically _____ is highly unlikely to happen. Logically_____ is never going to happen. Physically, it is impossible for _____ to happen.

Doesn't seem realistic, does it? Well guess what? Dead people should not come alive but reread Luke 8:49-52 and see what happened in Jairus' home. A child– that statistically, logically, and physically seemed all but dead– lived.

So can you. So can your situation. So can your marriage. So can your area of lack. So can your crazy teenage kids. So can your career in a tense situation. So can anything that you added in the "blanks." Life is available to you. But you must first believe that God can overcome the statistics. Belief is the prerequisite. God will not bless your disbelief. Belief can be your bridge to life. Believe today that God can and God will.

Being realistic is the most common path to mediocrity.

Will Smith

"NO" IS A COMPLETE SENTENCE

Grow a wise heart - you'll do yourself a favor; keep a clear head - you'll find a good life.

Proverbs 19:8, MSG

I used to think that being called a superwoman was a compliment. I would juggle a number of things at once successfully and I had a real problem with saying "no." I would throw on that cape and come to the rescue even if it meant that I was going to be burned out.

The cape is connected to self-image. We all have an image of ourselves and we also have what we want other people to think of us. My wiring is so much about helping other people and about love that I could never make "no" an assertive response. For such a long time part of my image was connected to being liked and wanting people to see me as being supportive. I enjoyed the thought of helping people figure out their problems and it made me feel good to see other people fulfilled, happy, and growing. Eventually, the superwoman image became so inextricably meshed with who I thought I really was that I would leap tall buildings in a single bound all while neglecting myself. I never said no if it meant that someone else would lack. There came a point where I had to start separating that image of superwoman from who I am as a human being.

I came to realize that I was just doing a long list of things, and although these lists benefited other people, they weren't always good for me. I wasn't as happy as the people I had overextended myself to help. I was often exhausted, depleted financially, and hurt when my efforts went unappreciated. There was no balance in that.

Paul, in 2 Cor 8:12-13, puts it this way: "For if the willingness is there, the gift is acceptable according to what one has, not according to what he does not have. Our desire is not that others might be relieved while you are hard pressed, but that there might be equality." Eventually I came to accept that superwoman is just a fictitious character. I started to peel away those layers of that image and I asked myself, "What does self love look like for a very real Halleemah?" The answer was simple – learning to say no.

For some men "no" empowers them to enter the space needed to accomplish goals. For many women, saying "no" is literally preaching a eulogy to martyrdom. I can speak personally to women readers in saying that some of us live our lives leading with our maternal instincts and have no sense of balance when it comes to self-care. We take pride in the sacrifices we make for our family, friends, jobs, partners, and children so much so that the thought of being selfish is likened to sin. However, to make a decision solely based on our own well being is something that God values greatly.

A heart that grows wise understands the true balance of loving God, loving our neighbors, and still accomplishing adequate self-love. Saying "no" is an act of self-love and not selfishness. Galatians 5:14 says, "For the whole law can be summed up in this one command: "Love your neighbor *as yourself*." This means that the love we give to others shouldn't leave us without any love left to give ourselves. If it does, then we are not truly following what Jesus taught to be one of the greatest commandments – love your neighbour *as yourself*. What would it look like for you to turn all of the care, love, and commitment that you give to others onto yourself? What would it look like for you to say no to others and yes to yourself? Embrace "no" as a complete sentence, for your own well being.

> *When you say 'Yes' to others, make sure you are not saying 'No' to yourself.*
> Paolo Coehlo

SING ABOUT ME... BUILDING OUR LEGACY

For I am already being poured out as a drink offering, and the time of my departure is at hand. I have fought the good fight, I have finished the race, I have kept the faith. Finally, there is laid up for me the crown of righteousness, which the Lord, the righteous judge, will award to me on that Day, and not only to me but also to all who have loved his appearing.

2 Timothy 4:6-8, NKJV

Admittedly, I am a bit of a Kendrick Lamar enthusiast. Kendrick Lamar is a young hip hop artist that burst onto the mainstream music scene after a series of extraordinary mix tapes. His music was embraced by urban neighborhoods for years before he was signed to a major record label. I listen to his music almost as much as I listened to Tupac Shakur as a teenager– which was a great deal.

Listening to Kendrick has been a way to connect with someone that can communicate artistically the heart of both my original place and my progression. His poetic delivery, commitment to being true to himself and his art, his simplistic yet brilliant ability to communicate his inner conflict with what it means to be a sinner with a desire for God, and of course his commitment to representing the city of Compton, have made me Kendrick's self proclaimed biggest fan.

My favorite Kendrick record that I play at least three to four times a week is somewhat of an urban translation of Paul's letter to Timothy in this passage. The song is called *Sing About Me...I'm Dying of Thirst*. He concludes the song by pointing out his desire to leave a legacy:

> Fighting for your rights, even when you're wrong
> And hope that at least one of you sing about me when I'm gone
> Am I worth it? Did I put enough work in?
>
> Promise that you will sing about me
> Promise that you will sing about me
>
> When the lights shine off and its my turn to settle down
> My main concern
> Is promise that you will sing about me
> Promise that you will sing about me

This song touches me in a special way every time that I hear it. Kendrick was purely communicating his desire to leave a legacy that would not only outlive the songs that he wrote, but also outlive the minutes, and seconds of his own life. I want to do the same.

In Paul's letter to Timothy, he parallels this sentiment. Paul was facing death. As a disciple of Christ, who "put enough work in," he had kept the faith and was ready for his crown. Paul was grateful for all of the people that God used him to touch along

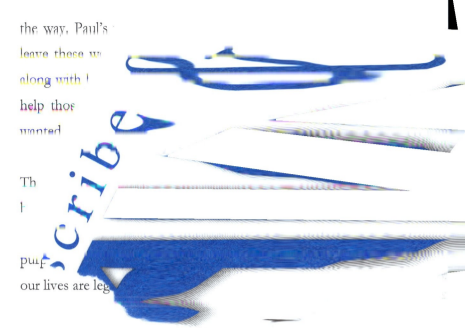

I consider this so frequently because in addition to living a life pleasing to God, I also want to live a life poured out. I want to leave this world having given my all, with no potential left. Like Kendrick, I want to be sure that I work to build a legacy for those to come.

All good men and women must take responsibility to create legacies that will take the next generation to a level we could only imagine.
Jim Rohn

VISION BOARDING

Write the vision, and make it plain upon tables, that he may run that readeth it. For the vision is yet for an appointed time, but at the end it shall speak, and not lie: though it tarry, wait for it; because it will surely come, it will not tarry.

Habakkuk 2:2-3, KJV

Vision boarding proved to be one of the most fun, creative, and faith supporting activities that I've done. Last year, during the holidays I was in a very discontent place. I felt God moving me in a different direction but I was unsure of where. I determined that this was actually a wonderful place to find myself. I was a blank canvas. I needed God's direction to help me understand the stirring in my spirit. In turn, I figured that the end of the year was a perfect time to vision board and write out all of the things that God was speaking to my heart as well as the things I had talked about doing for years but was never moved to action because I was too afraid. The cure to my confusion and my fear was vision boarding.

I am now an enthusiastic advocate of every person creating an annual or a seasonal vision board whenever God moves you to make changes in your lives. Real change takes some strategic thinking.

When you create your vision board, ask yourself concrete questions that stimulate your imagination. What have you been praying for? Where do you want to be? What does it look like? Who's there? What would the picture look like if there were no limits? As you consider the answers, write them down. Illustrate your thought process. This activity is all about visually proclaiming your next level. This isn't effective if it's just a collage of earthly desires. So, before you begin cutting out magazine photos of your favorite cars and destinations, ask yourself– where do I feel God leading me in this season of my life?

Prayer is critical. I encourage you to fast for a period of time as well. Go on a three or seven day fast. Step away from popular images and conversations with others about what you should do. Empty yourself of self, of popular opinion, and popular culture. Spend some time engulfed in God's presence. Overdo it! Afterwards, spend a Sunday after church with your Bible, and your vision board. What scripture passages did God lead you to? What colors seemed more vibrant? What thoughts gave you peace? What things should you consider putting on the chopping block of your life? What new things will be important additions to prepare you for your next level?

Goal setting is great, but a vision is much more specific. There is really something extra special about honing in on God's vision for your life and creating a visual representation of that. The mind will understand and gravitate toward what it sees. If it is merely a thought in your mind, there is a chance that it won't get past being just a powerful thought alone. Let your vision board stimulate your faith for what will soon be a present reality.

Go for it! Make vision boarding a necessary activity. Let your vision board guide you in this season. Proclaim your next level!

Visualize this thing you want. See it, feel it, believe in it. Make your mental blueprint and begin.

Robert Collier

PURPLE HEART

Not only so, but we also glory in our sufferings, because we know that suffering produces perseverance; perseverance, character; and character, hope. And hope does not put us to shame, because God's love has been poured out into our hearts through the Holy Spirit, who has been given to us.
Romans 5:3-5, NIV

I wondered why a Purple Heart medal was seen as a badge of honor. Why not a red heart? After all, a heart should be painted as bright and life giving. A heart is not meant to be a bruised color. It made no sense. I did some research, and the Purple Heart is awarded by the President of the United States to members of the United States Armed Forces who have been wounded or killed while in service. For those who live to receive this honor, the Purple Heart then, is a reward for survival of a near death experience in battle.

The life I live today has inspired and touched so many but it has been watered with so many tears and even lonely storms. In recent years, there have been painful challenges that have brought me to my knees in full submission to God's voice. It was only there on my knees that I heard Him fully, clearly, and with a heart empty enough to be filled with His complete love. Because of these instances, I have a stronger gratefulness for being both blessed and broken. As I think back on these storms, I see that God always produced something incredible on the other side. I've seen rainbows through my tears. After a tough breakup I started my own company. After the death of my grandfather, I mended severed relationships with family members whom I'd long written off. Following a medical scare, I trained and ran my first half marathon.

God pushes us forward and molds us into His image, and He uses whatever circumstances necessary to do so. God will even use scars, bruises, and painful situations to produce the perseverance we need to stimulate hope if that is what it takes to make us better Christians.

In the riveting Chris Cleave novel, *Little Bee*, the main character shares a painful story of her own wounds and says, "a scar is never ugly. We must see all scars as beauty. Because take it from me, a scar does not form on the dying. A scar means, I survived."

Pain stimulates growth especially if we are willing to accept the lesson. My heart may feel bruised but its survival through pain and turmoil has given its color character. The bruised heart is honorable and triumphant. It is even medal worthy. Now, for me, there is such beauty in the Purple Heart medal. I can see my storms and hard fought battles as triumphant gifts that elevated me into new levels of purpose. My heart, though bruised, is likened to that Purple Heart medal. A symbol of honor and a remembrance for the victories won.

Consider it pure joy, my brothers and sisters, whenever you face trials of many kinds, because you know that the testing of your faith produces perseverance. Let perseverance finish its work so that you may be mature and complete, not lacking anything.

James 1:2-4, NIV

FAIL BETTER

My flesh and my heart may fail, but God is the strength of my heart and my portion forever.

Psalm 73:26, NIV

Failure can bring about seasons of lull, which can drag on if we hold on to a warped understanding of loss. Our attitude towards failure is critical. For some, failure can be so debilitating that it negatively impacts relationships, careers, and ability to move forward in faith. When we let failure become poisonous then we are failing the wrong way. We have to learn to fail effectively.

Many of the great biblical figures in scripture like Abraham, Moses, David, and Peter experienced significant failure. However, those failures did not derail them completely or keep them from their purpose in God. If anything, it propelled them. Not only did they recover from failure but they also used it as an opportunity for personal development. This should help us to develop a healthier definition of failure. Regardless of the circumstances surrounding failure, all failure serves as a formidable tool equipped with important lessons.

It takes practice to fail effectively. Failure may feel like it is coming constantly for you, and if so, that may mean that you haven't learned what you need to in order to cross the bridge from failure to success. We learn through practice. Success requires a set of experiences, strength, and knowledge that can be gained through failure. Success also takes resilience. If you have ever fell flat on your face, like I have, then you have learned the value of the valley. The valley prepares you to reach the mountaintop. I have looked back at God's provision in what I perceived to be failure and all I can do is tell God thanks for it. Legendary investor Warren Buffett once said, "Everything in my life that looked like a failure turned into a success."

Failure reminds us of the consequences of our decisions. It helps us to create priorities. Yet, failure is only effective if we accept its teachings. Failure produces wisdom but failing to receive this wisdom can impact us negatively.

God will engineer failure to be the machine that produces success in your life. We may have to live with the consequences of some of our failure, but God's power and love are always available to us. David summed this up in Psalm 73 where he acknowledges his failure but also acknowledges God's power. We may fail but God is the strength of our hearts and our portion forever. A great scriptural dismissal of the incorrect perception of failure can be seen in Jude 1:24-25 which states, "To him who is able to keep you from falling and to present you before his glorious presence without fault and with great joy - to the only God our Savior be glory, majesty, power and authority, through Jesus Christ our Lord, before all ages, now and forevermore! Amen."

Face your failure, take the lessons, and grow from it. When you have a correct understanding of failure, you embrace it as a tool to help you grow. Let this understanding empower you to fail better.

> *Though fairy tales end after ten pages, our lives do not. We are multi-volume sets. In our lives, even though one episode amounts to a crash and burn, there is always another episode awaiting us and then another. There are always more opportunities to get it right, to fashion our lives in the ways we deserve to have them. Don't waste your time hating a failure. Failure is a greater teacher than success.*
>
> Clarissa Pinkola Estes

DEEPENED GRATITUDE

Rejoice always, pray without ceasing, in everything give thanks; for this is the will of God in Christ Jesus for you.

1 Thessalonians 5:16-18, NKJV

We are commanded to give thanks in all things. Whether it's a situation that tries us or one that blesses us dramatically– we are called to be thankful.

As easy as it sounds, I lose sight of this repeatedly. I know this because I actually conducted a complaining experiment. I decided to mark down in my task application on my iPhone how many times I complained about something throughout the day. In the week that I conducted this experiment, I didn't go a single day without complaining about something. I complained about traffic, long lines at the grocery store, a client that showed up late, bad customer service, and dropped calls on my cellular phone. Truthfully, we are all guilty of complaining. Even the happiest people in the world can find themselves murmuring without even realizing it.

After a week of complaint inventory, I committed to spend 5 minutes at the start of every day writing down a list of things I was grateful for. The list was new every day. Some days, it was hard to get through my list without weeping. This was such a sobering exercise. When I went beyond thanking God for the basics— my job, my family, and my friends— I would think about things that I often take for granted. I recognized that my complaints were trivial. I thanked God for the ability to hear music, for sight without corrective lenses, and for coats to shield my skin from cold. I praised God for the ability to read, for access to clean water, for the movement of my limbs without assistance, for access to medicine when I got sick and food when I was hungry.

The following week I used this list as a notice to stop complaining. I made a conscious decision to stop sweating the small stuff because, in all honesty, every breath is a new reason to be grateful.

This changed how I prayed. When I considered the magnitude of God's blessings in every second of every day I was motivated to aspire to achieve consistent gratefulness. Now, I try to be as intentional as I can about giving thanks to God for all that I've been granted and for all that God means to me.

I heard a minister tell a story once about his own inability to be consistently grateful. He said that if he had one wish he would ask for a greater ability to appreciate all that he already had. What a powerful wish.

I ask you, as I ask myself, where is your sense of thankfulness? How complete is it? How deep does it run in your life? How mindful are you of ungrateful behavior? How committed are you to being more grateful today than you were yesterday?

Enter his gates with thanksgiving

and his courts with praise;

give thanks to him and praise his name.

For the LORD *is good and his love endures forever;*

his faithfulness continues through all generations.

PSALM 100:4-5, NIV

DISCIPLINE IN MONEY MANAGEMENT

Whoever disregards discipline comes to poverty and shame, but whoever heeds correction is honored
                                                                Proverbs 13:18, NIV

So much is said about the importance of healthy body image, character in business, physical wellness, and service to others, but we forget that money management is also an act of stewardship.

A few years ago, shortly after starting my postgraduate independence I needed a number of big ticket items. These purchases appeared hard to acquire while staring at student loan debt and a terrible credit score. I had a decision to make. At the time, I thought the answer was picking up a few more jobs but what I needed required more than that. This was about discipline. It was time to reframe how I viewed tithing, spending, and budgeting. I needed to learn how to do much with little, and exercise obedience when it came to my money management decisions.

My church was having a 21-day spending fast in which I decided to take things a bit further and stretch my fasting to 90 days. During the fast, I cut out frivolous spending, dining out, and any expense that was not out of absolute necessity. I elected to do my hair at home instead of going to the salon, I learned how to perfect do-it-yourself manicures on YouTube, I became a professional at coupon shopping, and I incorporated more modest eating habits. I meticulously budgeted every dime of my income and committed to spending a full year obedient to tithing without any weeks where I used the "I will catch back up next week" excuse.

I sat down with a financial advisor, who was also my mentor at the time, to sort through my credit, savings plan, retirement, and my weekly spending. Having a financial advisor proved to be an incredible asset in this process. She helped me to think about money wisely. It wasn't necessarily about being rich. Instead, it was about having a healthy understanding of money management and wealth creation within the confines of my own income and budgeting. I also learned to give personal finance the correct focus. To help me give money its proper place in my thinking, my advisor would habitually say, "Money can buy you a boat but it cannot ensure smooth sailing. It can buy a big wedding but it cannot give you a good marriage."

Finally, I spent time in prayer and in study of God's Word. A lot of this process was about undoing bad habits that I had developed over time. Having no real financial education, I had been conditioned to try to make as much money as I could and figure out how to spend it. There was no real commitment to savings. To put it bluntly, I was just bad with money.

I spent time in scripture just hoping to understand what the biblical portrait of money management looked like. Whether it was understanding the commandment to tithe (Deuteronomy 14:22, Proverbs 3:9-10) or how we should view and manage debt (Romans 13:8), the portrait I saw in scripture was one painted with disciplined thinking.

I came out of my 90 spending fast with a financial plan that I committed to for the remainder of the year. My fast, and the time I spent with my financial advisor, helped me reach my goal. I paid off my credit card debt, improved my credit score, and developed a weekly budget that contributed to an overall better financial position for both the present and the future. Disciplined thinking led me to good stewardship. Some of you may have financial goals that seem inaccessible. Maybe your solution is better discipline.

Moreover, it is required in stewards that they be found faithful.

1 Corinthians 4:2, ESV

EACH ONE, REACH ONE

The unfolding of your words gives light; it imparts understanding to the simple.

Psalm 119:130, ESV

When life's tests bring me to a place where I have no understanding and no response, I turn to the words of the experienced. Langston Hughes in his poem *Mother to Son*, illustrates the wisdom of experience in a conversation between a mother and her son:

> *Well, son, I'll tell you.*
> *Life for me ain't been no crystal stair.*
> *It's had tacks in it,*
> *And splinters,*
> *And boards torn up,*
> *And places with no carpet on the floor --Bare.*
> *But all the time I'se been a-climbin' on...*
> *So boy, don't you turn back.*
> *Don't you set down on the steps*
> *'Cause you finds it's kinder hard.*
> *Don't you fall now*
> *For I'se still goin', honey,*
> *I'se still climbin',*
> *And life for me ain't been no crystal stair.*

In this poem, a very wise mother educates her son on the importance of perseverance in this rocky walk of life. Here is a woman who could reach back even as she climbed because she knew about wanting to give up, and about the painful trek upward when you feel like you're being pulled down. This mother was pouring the wisdom of experience into her son. Through relationship, she was able to make clear what it meant to be called to climb those stairs, and never quit even when there was little will to climb. She was mentoring her son.

Although the word "mentor" isn't mentioned explicitly in the Bible the principles are found all throughout scripture. Moses was a mentor to Joshua, Elijah to Elisha, and Jesus mentored the disciples. These examples demonstrate how our words and instruction can light the path for others.

Mentorship is how we go beyond words to actually shifting paradigms.

This is especially important for our current generation of young people. Mentorship helps our children to dream. Mentorship is our active prayer that asks God to use us as a vessel. It is through mentorship that young people can reclaim their ability to dream. Through a mentoring relationship, we help others not only dream but also determine what it takes to make those dreams come true. It is important that youth see themselves reflected in the people who are teaching them. We have to see mentorship as a critical component to shaping what our future looks like. It has been an amazing gift for me to mentor teens and use my experience as a guiding foundation. I have seen, first hand, how a mentor can provide blueprints and be an example of success.

Although the mother to son relationship in this poem is one of "motherly" mentorship it is vital that we have the same level of care and motivation for the countless lost people who are crying out for guidance and leadership. A worthy response is for all of us to reach at least one of them.

Our fingertips never fade from the lives we touch.

Mahatma Gandhi

REST IN GOD'S COMPLETE CARE

When you pass through the waters, I will be with you; and when you pass through the rivers, they will not sweep over you. When you walk through the fire, you will not be burned; the flames will not set you ablaze. For I am the LORD your God… you are precious and honored in my sight, and because I love you…

Isaiah 43:2-4, NIV

A few years ago, while traveling to Haiti, I experienced one of the most enchanting moments of my life. In the mountain village of Fondwa, I, along with other volunteers, spent time with children who were living in an orphanage. The culmination of the trip was our opportunity to drive the children to a beach area called Jacmel. We loaded an open bed truck and squeezed in the children and the group leaders. We drove up an unpaved road that was narrow and rocky. Because the children were not used to riding in a moving vehicle many of them got motion sickness.

To be candid, the drive was terrifying. But, as we drove, I set aside my concerns in order to comfort the three young girls that I held in my arms. Although I have a small body frame, I managed to hold all three of them. I literally had a child on each knee and one on my lap. They felt so comfortable that, in spite of the shaky journey, they closed their eyes and rested for most of the ride. That moment, holding those young girls through a rocky and dangerous ride, was an eternal moment. I will remember it forever. Although I thought the ride should have made them fearful, they trusted me enough to rest in my arms without fear of the outside world. We were headed to the beach where they could spend the day away from the orphanage just playing in the water and having fun. They trusted me to be that bridge of security from the orphanage to the ocean.

I want to have the same trust in God's care. I want to trust that no matter how rocky the road, God is not only with me, but He is holding me in His care. At times we have the impression that we are holding on to God's unchanging hand but it is really God who is holding on to ours.

I think that we would worry a lot less if we understood the truth of Isaiah 43:2-4. It's easy to worry when we embrace the nihilistic sensibility that we have control over everything. In truth, we do not have control over most things. Most things that happen are outside the realm of our control. There are trials that we will have to face and battles that we must enter but regardless of the gravity of that space – we must remember that we are in God's complete care.

Whenever I feel far from God, this passage reminds me how close God always is. God has promised to never leave us, so the stress that we have is meaningless when placed against this passage. Overcoming waters? Flames? Danger? No problem. God has me in His complete care. I am precious to Him.

Like those little girls, I can always rest comfortably on the road from where I have been to destinations unforeseen.

In sickness or in health, sanity or in madness, in the vigor of youth or in the decrepitude of senility, God speaks these words which he spoke once to Augustine: 'Run, I will carry you, I will bring you to the end of your journey and there also I will carry you.

Maurice O'Connor Drury, The Danger Of Words

LEADERSHIP INTERCESSION

I urge, then, first of all, that petitions, prayers, intercession and thanksgiving be made for all people—for kings and all those in authority, that we may live peaceful and quiet lives in all godliness and holiness. This is good, and pleases God our Savior...

1 Timothy 2:1-3, NIV

The best part of my day is getting phone calls and random loving text messages from my friends. It is the best feeling in the world. I get so inundated with meetings reminders, speaking requests, networking emails, and project proposals that I find so much joy when people support me and check to see how I am doing personally. It is a double blessing to hear that my friends are praying for me. Even Paul requested prayer in Romans 15:30: "Now I beg you, brethren, through the Lord Jesus Christ, and through the love of the Spirit, that you strive together with me in your prayers to God for me." I am grateful for those prayers because I acknowledge how important they are in the world of leadership.

It's tough to watch when leaders are denied the latitude granted to the rest of humanity. CEOs shouldn't steal money, husbands and wives shouldn't commit infidelity, politicians should be honest, and professional athletes should not take performance-enhancing drugs. But in the real world, these things happen all the time. How leaders bounce back from their own mistakes is connected to the community that supports them.

In 1 Timothy 2, Paul instructs us to pray for our leaders. We are instructed to pray so that "we may live peaceful and quiet lives in all godliness and holiness."

How much time do you commit to prayer for those who lead you in your life? How much do you pray for your boss, your pastor, your bible study leader, your trainer, your mentor, or your professors? They too, are human, and susceptible to brokenness. There must be an effort to uplift and not tear down those who take up leadership roles and work to bear the cross in ministry. I am an ordained minister and I still fall short just as much as the next person. Does that discredit me from deserving your prayers? Carrying the cross does not make anyone perfect. It makes one hungry for perfection. If prayer time got as much air as gossip, then there might be much less weakened leaders.

All of us have God sized holes but some people also have church sized scars. Some have been hurt by those who administer the gospel, making it understandable that so many have little comfort with what's going on within the churches' walls. Our hurt supports our ease in taking positions on the side of religious spite. There has to be a healing of our hearts and a departure from thinking we are anything more than human beings trying to get this whole life thing right.

Christian leaders are in a vulnerable position and need a greater concentration of prayer and intercession because of their level of responsibility. Public visibility makes them more subject to criticism should they make mistakes. Paul declares that prayer for leadership is not an option, but a necessity.

As a community, we stand to benefit from praying for leaders. Prayer and intercession for leadership releases God's plan for the communities they lead and the projects they support. Praying for leadership can cause a positive change in their effectiveness and in the effectiveness of their work.

The most underutilized source of spiritual power in our churches today is the intercession for Christian leaders.

C. Peter Wagner, The Prayer Shield

HOW FOOLISH OF ME

Brothers and sisters, think of what you were when you were called. Not many of you were wise by human standards; not many were influential; not many were of noble birth. But God chose the foolish things of the world to shame the wise; God chose the weak things of the world to shame the strong. God chose the lowly things of this world and the despised things— and the things that are not—to nullify the things that are, so that no one may boast before him… "Let the one who boasts boast in the Lord."

1 Corinthians 1:26-31, NIV

Boy was I rough around the edges in high school. I really had no sense of appropriation when it came to acquiring what I needed. I was reading my old diary and I will summarize an entry that I stumbled upon that may help me to visualize this point.

On occasion, when I didn't have money, I would go around and take random collections for a nail to get repaired, bus fare home, lunch, or whatever I needed at the time. One afternoon, in history class, my teacher stepped out of the classroom and I saw an open opportunity and stood in front of the class and asked, "Does anybody got any money on my fill? My nail is broke." Although I was completely serious, the classroom erupted in laughter. The teacher returned to my mid-day fundraising attempt and asked me to stay after class. He warned me that what I was doing could be considered peddling and I would be sent to the principal's office if it happened again. "Whatever, I thought. My nail is broken, and I need to get it fixed. Hey, I still have the after school let out to collect. And collect I did. $11. Bus fare and a nail fill. Success."

It's difficult to look back at that diary entry and not be completely embarrassed. I must have looked so silly to people. This continued in college but the difference is, I channeled my efforts into college level business ventures. I styled hair, I sold dinners, I rented a car and created an airport shuttle during holiday breaks, and I also had a laundry service. I have always been a hustler at heart. Over the years I have watched God fine tune what was once foolish teenage behavior into an ongoing tenacity that paved the way for the entrepreneurial endeavors that would come. I started in my high school hallways hustling people out of money and now I own a business and excel at contract negotiations.

God will use what may be seem like a weakness for His ultimate glory. In 1 Corinthians 1 we are taught that "God chose the foolish things of the world to shame the wise, and God chose the weak things of the world to shame the strong." God will grant us ordinary gifts and bless us with extraordinary purpose. This way, we cannot boast in ourselves but we become arrows that point to the cross.

You may be insecure about certain characteristics that seem foolish to other people. You may feel unusual and you may even see your weaknesses as negatives. Do not discredit them. They may be the tools that God wants to use as building blocks for His purpose.

Many biblical leaders chosen by God didn't make logical sense. They weren't worthy according to the world's standards, yet God chose them. Moses was a shepherd whose daily work consisted of leading sheep around but God used Moses and his shepherding skill to lead his people to the Promised Land. Esther was a slave but God used her to save her people from being massacred. Matthew was a tax collector but used his record keeping skills to write one of the Gospels that told the story of the life of Jesus. In present day, when reading the stories of Nelson Mandela, Steve Jobs, Ellen Johnson Sirleaf, and Oprah Winfrey- you will find giants that started with a dream and an unusual skill or a character weakness. What's your hustle? What's your foolish trait?

I'm a hustler homie

Jay Z

LEADERSHIP IN THE WORKPLACE

Shepherd the flock of God that is among you, exercising oversight, not under compulsion, but willingly, as God would have you; not for shameful gain, but eagerly; not domineering over those in your charge, but being examples to the flock.

1 Peter 5:2-3, NAS

One of the best parts about being an entrepreneur in the world of sports philanthropy is having the opportunity to employ aspiring professionals. Employing interns and project staff often translates into mentoring relationships. These relationships have the potential to serve as a bridge in the journey to secure a full time position in sports. Professional sports is a tough industry to crack into and the more experience that candidates have the more competitive they become.

Recently, I sat down with one of my interns for their end of term review and was shown the vast opportunity that leaders have as illustrated in 1 Peter 5:2-3. When I asked this certain young lady what the best part of her experience was, I thought she would mention the excitement of working in a fast paced environment, or the opportunity to contribute to fundraising for athlete related charities, or the hands on event experience. These are usually a popular response for college interns. Instead, she began to run down experiences that would be memorable outside of the obvious resume bullet points.

She talked about an instance when the team traveled off site for lunch and I gave food to a homeless man. She highlighted being moved when one of the professional athletes prayed over the meal during a funder lunch. I listened to how impacted she was by how leadership managed conflict in tense situations. She pointed out that she took note of how I led by example from my attire to being courteous to people in every level of external organizations. She even mentioned how pleasant our receptionist was and how it set the pace for the day.

This was an unusual review because I felt more like a pupil than a teacher. My intern was teaching me about the power of the kind of executive leadership that extends beyond the boardroom in providing a meaningful summer experience. In leadership, we are not only responsible for creating the kind of environment that brings out the best in people but we are also visible examples of the things we hope to inspire through our words.

Of course I wanted to impart my own pillars of successful interning: personal brand is paramount, position yourself in a way that you are always looking to develop yourself as a professional and your organization, build your reputation in bad situations, remember to keep your integrity. Yet, there were even louder lessons that I imparted without being conscious of it. Although this was a complimentary conversation I couldn't help but wonder how many times I responded negatively and didn't serve as a good witness. It was a humbling reminder that I am called to live as Jesus instructed in Matthew 5:16, "Let your light shine before men in such a way that they may see your good works, and glorify your Father who is in heaven." How did I treat the poor? What kind of conversations was I overheard having? Was I building or breaking down? How was I seen resolving conflict? In leadership, our lifestyle is a powerful way to connect what we say to what's actionable.

Good leadership points to the message of the cross.

Leadership is lifting a person's vision to high sights, the raising of a person's performance to a higher standard, the building of a personality beyond its normal limitations.

Peter F. Drucker

FASHIONED IN VINTAGE

O LORD, you have searched me and known me! You know when I sit down and when I rise up; you discern my thoughts from afar. You search out my path and my lying down and are acquainted with all my ways. Even before a word is on my tongue, behold, O LORD, you know it altogether. You hem me in, behind and before, and lay your hand upon me. Such knowledge is too wonderful for me; it is high; I cannot attain it.

For you formed my inward parts; you knitted me together in my mother's womb. I praise you, for I am fearfully and wonderfully made. Wonderful are your works; my soul knows it very well. My frame was not hidden from you when I was being made in secret, intricately woven in the depths of the earth.

Psalm 139:1-6 and 13-15, ESV

My favorite fashion blog is a site called The Werk! Place. The blogger behind The Werk! Place is a mix master at merging the old and new and making it current and attractive. In today's world of mass media and globalization we struggle to be current in ways that cause us to lose our true sense of self and often our self worth. It is so important that we have a balanced concept of a healthy sense of self. That is why I love vintage fashion. It is a great sermonic analogy for a balanced sense of self worth. Vintage fashion does not waiver or change. It prompts you to bring it into your current season, unaffected by time, as an enduring piece. It makes you catch up to it instead of the other way around. Isn't that what sense of self really is?

Vintage speaks also to value, because the acquisition of vintage items can yield a promising return on investment in the future. God sees tremendous value in us. We are God's vintage and valuable investment. Ironically, there is a temptation to allow circumstances, and what's currently within our sight, to make us believe that certain things happen because we have no value. Quite the contrary. Let nothing shake your belief that you are valuable. All that takes places in your life – both wonderful and difficult – takes place *because* you are valuable. It's so counter intuitive. The truth of the gospel reveals that God fashioned us with purpose and a remarkable plan and that plan has incredible worth to God.

We are of so much value that the hairs of our head are numbered (Luke 12:17). When discussing the concept of worrying, Jesus reminds us to "Look at the birds of the air; they do not sow or reap or store away in barns, and yet your heavenly Father feeds them. "Are you not much more valuable than they (Matthew 6:26)?" If we view our self worth through the eyes of Jesus we see how much we are loved, valued, and considered priceless. He called us both His beloved (John 1:12), and His friend (John 15:15).

Our worth in God's eyes is age old. It's vintage. When I lose sight of my self worth, I love to read David's analogy of God as the quintessential tailor. In Psalm 139, David says that we are "intricately woven." Each one of us is unique and designed very specifically. God's purpose and blessings for me are haute couture. They are exclusively custom fit.

It is difficult to make a man miserable while he feels worthy of himself and claims kindred to the great God who made him.

Abraham Lincoln

A WORLD WORTHY OF ITS CHILDREN

Let us rise up and build.

Nehemiah 2:18, NKJV

One of the most beautiful and amazing little girls in this world is Kendall Simone Parks. I may be a little biased, as she is the child that I am blessed to co-Godparent. I have a birds eye view of her parents investing love and time into her everyday. It is a marvelous thing to watch and support.

When Kendall was still in her mother's womb I committed to spend some time in prayer for her (1 Samuel 1:27-28). My prayer time was along the backdrop of multiple tragic news stories that made me much more sensitive to just how vulnerable children are. Watching these calamities in the news cycle shined a light on the importance of not only praying for Kendall and her parents throughout her life, but also building roads that would make her future a bright place to grow up.

We live in a broken world that seems beyond repair. It doesn't take much research to see the interminable sea of social ills and communities of people that live in pain. The Book of Nehemiah shows us that in the face of despair, faith can remove barriers and restore broken walls. We are called to actively engage in the betterment of our society. We are called to build.

How many of us have wept at unfair verdicts but have never written to our elected representatives? How many of us have been pained by poverty but have never been moved to action? How many of us have become desensitized to violence and unplugged from the needs of those that Jesus called "the of the least of these?" How much has mass incarceration, hunger, homelessness, poverty and lack of access to basic human necessities, and substandard classrooms become commonplace?

I keep a photo of Kendall on my office desk and on my home refrigerator to remind me of the task that I have. The task to build a wonderful world for her and for all of my nieces, nephews, and the children whose faces I've seen all around the globe. It's a responsibility that we all have. Legislative advocacy is not just for aspiring politicians. Mentorship is not exclusive to the wildly successful, and fighting for the provision of human rights is not just for those who consider themselves activists. Engaging in political discourse doesn't mean that we are blurring the lines of church and state. It means we are exercising our voices and fighting for a better world for our children (Nehemiah 4:14).

Pablo Casals, a world renowned musician communicated this beautifully when he said, "we must all work to make the world worthy of its children." What kind of world are we building for our children? What kind of world will I contribute to for

Kendall Parks? My hope is that I can build like Nehemiah in the face of what seems to be overwhelming despair.

Be active.

Build.

You will rebuild those houses left in ruins for years; you will be known as a builder and repairer of city walls and streets.

Isaiah 58.12, CEV

READY? SET? CHILL.

Be anxious for nothing, but in everything by prayer and supplication, with thanksgiving, let your requests be made known to God; and the peace of God, which surpasses all understanding, will guard your hearts and minds through Christ Jesus.

Philippians 4:6-7, NKJV

After years of speaking on singles panels and young adult workshops throughout the country, I have a resounding prayer request and it is for God to send down a widespread healing for what is called "the thirst." We are just so anxious for what we want that we can lose sight of God's consistent presence in our lives, our faith, and in some instances, even our self- respect.

We have all been guilty of being thirsty at some point. Some of us more intensely than others. Thankfully, Philippians 4:6-7 provides a remedy for parched throats everywhere. Don't be overly anxious. Pray. God will grant you an overwhelming peace and contentment for exactly where you are while you await the coming of your not yet.

For example, singles have a tendency to romanticize what it is to be married the same way couples, who have been married for long periods of time, romanticize about being single. Single people are anxious to get married. Certain married couples are anxious to have kids. Once married couples have children, many are anxious for some silent time away from their children. Parents of teenagers are anxious to be empty nesters. Employed people are anxious to get a job. People that hate their jobs spend Monday through Friday reiterating how anxious they are to make it to the weekend. Anxiousness can be an all-consuming emotion that is the exact opposite of peace.

Being anxious for nothing simply means never letting the things that you *want* make you uneasy and forgetful of the things you *have*. It means that prayer and contentment helps us not to lose sight of where we are. It means not being consumed with what is completely beyond our control. If we could only find God's complete love and provision in our current space then we would spend less time being thirsty and we'd put our bodies through much less stress.

To this end, my prayer is that God burn in my recognition the loving, complete and redeeming God that exists in my right now. I want God to bless me with an overwhelming contentment. Prayer and serenity is a cure for the thirsty.

Psalm 51:17 says that "heart-shattered lives that think they are ready for love don't for a moment escape God's notice." You are not ready. You are just anxious. There's a difference.

Halleemah Nash, Women's Bible Study

FENG SHUI YOUR FRIENDSHIPS

Do not be misled: "Bad company corrupts good character."
1 Corinthians 15:33, NIV

In business, the saying, "your network is your net worth" is used all the time. It is certainly an vital practice to develop relationships that enhance our ability and grow our social capital, but our circle of friends is equally impactful. Friendships permeate our lives and impact our personal growth, stability, strength, career, family and even our health. Friends can contribute positive things to every area of our lives. Conversely, the wrong kinds of friends can deplete all areas of our lives if we allow them to.

Our associations are important (1 Corinthians 15:33) and we are blessed when we choose the right counsel (Psalm 1:1). Further, our inclination to behave wisely or foolishly is deeply connected to our companionships (Proverbs 13:20).

At a certain point in my adult life I had to do a relationship inventory. I took stock of all my close relationships and realized that there were toxic friendships that lingered in my life for years but weren't adding value. Toxic friendships are stressful, unreliable, and don't give anything back. These are the friendships that leave us questioning ourselves; and, they are void of the mutual support that is the byproduct of a healthy interaction.

I made the decision to feng shui my relationships. Toxic friendships had to be removed and healthy relationships had to be nurtured. In doing so, I hoped to create a friendship environment that developed my inner being and didn't deplete me mentally. As a result, my circle became more like a Cheerio. I realized that although I was surrounded by numerous people all of the time; everyone did not fit the description of "friend." Not everyone deserved a front seat in my journey. I had to start being smarter about who I hung out with and who I allowed to pour into my life. What I needed was a circle of the right *kind* of friends. Toxic friendships can drain the life out of you. The right friendships are life giving.

After my feng shui project, I began the work of deepening the interpersonal relationships that added value to my life and that mattered the most to me. The deepening of interpersonal relationships is such a critical piece to balanced living. We make room for so much in life but sometimes friendships take a back seat. I encourage you to reverse this trend by making valuable and personal relationships a priority. Once this took primacy for me, it became a regular practice to take time out after my workday to check on a friend's parents, or call one of my girlfriends to wish them a good day. I made time to text my guys to talk trash about sports and exchange pleasantries about the latest foolish news. I have become much better at remembering important dates in my friend's lives and seeing my friendships as my most valuable treasure. My friends take such wonderful care of my heart. They know what I need without me having to ask and they are accepting of me along with every one of my annoying flaws. They are worthy of investment.

In the world of networking and professional conquest I am learning to invest equal time in to the strengthening of interpersonal relationships that mean most. I don't want to be the kind of person that can remember phone numbers from business cards I received weeks ago but can't remember birthdays of those who are closest to me. How many of us place "being a better friend" in our 5-year plan?

My friends are my estate

Emily Dickenson

A DEVO FOR THE TRAVELER BEE... GOD IN SIGHTS AND STRUCTURE

The earth is the LORD's, and the fullness thereof; the world, and they that dwell therein,
For he hath founded it upon the seas, and established it upon the floods.

Psalm 24:1-2, KJV

In middle school I participated in a three-day camp program for urban youth and it was the first time I heard birds chirping in the morning, watched fish swimming in their natural habitat, and saw the stars bright and clear at night. Even as a young girl I saw the blessing in stepping away from my everyday norm to be energized by a new space. It gave me a thirst for life and a new way of seeing the world beyond stars and fish. In travel, I received a revived outlook. I have never been the same after experiencing the exhilaration of travel and new space. It even showed me new lessons.

Psalm 24 declares that the earth belongs to the Lord and I have read it time and time again, but it was not until I was blessed with opportunities to travel internationally that I could really connect with the second part that speaks to "the fullness thereof." Travel introduced me to the grand landscape of God's diverse creations.

In touring new places I saw God in bridges in California, bodies of water in Spain, sunrises in Haiti, food and wine in France, cobblestone in South America, ruins in Rome, rest in Jamaica, and foliage in Virginia. Travel allows us to open our eyes to God's work. And each new place changed me after.

Travel is one of the best forms of education. There are particular lessons that I didn't learn fully until I was removed from my comfort zone. I had to become geographically relocated for certain scriptures and truths to come alive.

One example is my interpretation of Psalm 63:1. The New Living Translation of this passage reads:

> My soul thirsts for you; my whole body longs for you in this parched and weary land where there is no water.

This transformed into powerful visual truth after I participated in a water walk in Africa. During this walk, I traveled with people who journey for miles to access water in remote villages. I also participated in prayer time with these same people who went days even weeks without water. I saw how a thirsting soul can be satisfied with God in the midst of water scarcity. Psalm 63;1 was given life through this experience. This impacted me so much that I made small changes without even considering it intentionally. My showers were shorter and my thoughts about water, and worship in the midst of lack, were forever enlightened.

Every new travel opportunity instantly became a sermon being preached, or a benediction being prayed, or a worship song being lifted.

I encourage you too to see God in news ways. Have an adventure. Start locally. Go on a neighborhood tour, or try a new restaurant. See a movie or a documentary in a different language. Ride a bike instead of taking the bus and take in your surroundings. Then, learn about the wonders of the world. If you don't have a passport, get one. Enlarge your mind with a new experience. See the fullness of God in sights and structures. When you return, you will be granted the gift of new sight, possibility, and another level of gratefulness for God as Creator.

I see God's power and His artisan in His creations. As a traveler, I experienced God minister to me in a more extraordinary way.

Travel is more than the seeing of sights; it is a change that goes on, deep and permanent, in the ideas of living.

Miriam Beard

RE-IMAGINING SUFFERING

Beloved, do not be surprised at the fiery ordeal that is taking place among you to test you, as though something strange were happening to you. But rejoice insofar as you are sharing Christ's sufferings so that you may also be glad and shout for joy when his glory is revealed. If you are reviled for the name of Christ, you are blessed, because the spirit of glory is revealed.

1 Peter 4:12-14, ISV

There are days when I wonder if God literally had a conversation with the devil and asked, "Well, have you considered my servant Halleemah?" At some point in this discipleship voyage, we will all be faced with some form of suffering. It may even be a suffering that causes us to go far past our breaking points in unimaginable, unexplainable, and inescapable ways.

Suffering can be more difficult to manage if we don't understand its purpose. We are connect with the story of Jesus the healer, comforter and protector, but not enough with the suffering servant. Most of us gravitate toward scripture lessons related to our satisfaction more than those that necessitate trails. In general, we have developed a warped understanding of suffering. We have been socialized to link suffering to evil, which prompts us to look for the easiest way out. We live in a pain killer culture that is filled with prescriptions, procedures and "how to" books that help of rid ourselves of pain and discomfort. This all makes a balanced understanding of suffering difficult to achieve.

Despite everything that the Bible says about the struggles of righteous people, some of us think that if we pray enough that God will remove all trials from our lives. Not so.

Here, Peter gives us a remedy for our misunderstanding of suffering. Re-imagine it. Do not be surprised at suffering because it is not alien to those in communion with the Christ, who also had to suffer. When we are confronted with the necessity of suffering, rejoice in it because of its relationship to glory. Peter was a witness to the sufferings of Christ as well as a participant of His glory.

To really endorse the concept of serving a suffering Christ is to embrace the entire story of Jesus. Serving Christ does not give us the option of merely embracing the portions that keep us comfortable. Suffering provides the occasion for us to participate in Jesus' entire story, not only His passion but also the promise of glory at the end of the story. When we undergo suffering, we share in the communion of Christ's suffering. It is important to have this kind of balanced story in order to meet the challenges of today's crises.

Re-imagine your own suffering, and it will allow you to see that suffering is the path to glory. It is a foretaste. Today we suffer but when Christ returns we will share in that glory. It is because of this re-imagining that Christians can "rejoice." In the end, we will participate in the glory of Christ.

Believe that there is a glory after this. This is why Peter rounds out this statement with a short doxology, "To him be the power forever and ever, Amen."

We are always on the anvil; by trials God is shaping us for higher things.

Henry Ward Beecher

WORTH THE WAIT

I remain confident of this: I will see the goodness of the Lord in the land of the living. Wait for the Lord; be strong and take heart and wait for the Lord.
Psalm 27: 13-14, NIV

I am not the most patient person in the world. I am always coming from somewhere or going to somewhere. Patience feels too much like standing still without enough movement for my taste. Despite this opinion, waiting on our "ultimate" is an active process. Waiting is an action that essentially points forward. This is a practical therapy for my consistent impatience.

What have you grown impatient about? What have you settled for out of your own impatience? What are you waiting for? Is it a job promotion? Is it a relationship? Is it a new level of life? Is it welcoming children into your happy marriage? Is it your college acceptances?

Whatever it is, God is calling our attention to this scripture to remind us that these things take time. The blessings of God are mighty and incredible and the level that God has for us is worth the wait. Therefore, wait in faith. Faith is the channel that connects us from the waiting to God's perfectly timed promise. David says in Psalm 27, "I remain confident of this: I will see the goodness of the Lord in the land of the living. Wait for the

Lord; be strong and take heart and wait for the Lord." It takes strength of heart to wait and David was confident in his hope. This confidence fueled his assurance that he was moving towards something better.

We are never forgotten. God is with us and His heart is for us. We may not like standing still but in waiting we are yet in God's care. If there is something that I do not have, it is because either I am not ready for it yet or it just is not for me to have at all. The process of waiting is often designed to protect us from what will likely destroy us if we acquire it prematurely. Submit to being under construction until you are ready to receive what you are waiting for.

In my balancing act I learned to rest in waiting. They that wait on the Lord shall renew their strength and mount up in wings like eagles. And we want eagle wings. We want to soar. Just wait. If you have literally felt destroyed by life's trials or felt railroaded as you await God's healing, please remember that His timing is perfect. If it seems slow, just wait patiently. It won't be delayed. It will come at the perfect time.

> *But these things I plan won't happen right away. Slowly, steadily, surely, the time approaches when the vision will be fulfilled. If it seems slow, wait patiently, for it will surely take place. It will not be delayed.*
>
> Habakkuk 2:3-4, NLT

SALTY – RELEASE FROM OUR PAST

Likewise also as it was in the days of Lot; they did eat, they drank, they bought, they sold, they planted, they builded; But the, same day that Lot went out of Sodom it rained fire and brimstone from heaven, and destroyed them all. Even thus shall it be in the day when the Son of man is revealed. In that day, he which shall be upon the housetop, and his stuff in the house, let him not come down to take it away: and he that is in the field, let him likewise not return back. Remember Lot's wife.

Luke 17:28-32, KJV

In Luke 17, Jesus is recapping the story of Lot's wife. She was turned into a pillar of salt after she defied God's warning. In an act of disobedience, she looked back at the city of Sodom, a city that was being destroyed by God. Jesus closes this passage with a short statement, "Remember Lot's wife." Even though it was a simple assertion, Jesus uses this simplicity to makes a powerful and dramatic point. Our ability to fully move forward and leave behind the destruction that exists in our past is critical. When Lot's wife turned and watched the flames consume everything from her former life–that decision in turn, consumed her.

It is not an easy feat to escape the former life that God is calling us to leave behind us. There are places in our past that are full of mistakes, pain, and missteps. These places can make us bitter, afraid, and salty. Focusing on this kind of past can become a soul prison. When we consider how easily it can shackle our faith and our forward progression, we see why Jesus singles out this truth in His sermon.

The original Hebrew translation for the words "looked back" in this passage indicates that she did more than take a short glance. These words mean to consider, or to take a longing look upon something. This is what Lot's wife did. She longed for a terminated city. Is your focus on your past really a longing for what was meant to be destroyed in your life? Release yourself from whatever is causing you to constantly look back at what God has deemed done and move forward!

In my personal prayers, I've had to ask God to discipline my mind so that I do not focus on the things of old so intensely that I am unable to fully experience today. I have constantly relived moments from my past in ways that made it difficult to believe God for my today. But, today is new. Time keeps moving. I have learned that I cannot reclaim yesterday. I can only learn the lessons and let it power me to live in today.

We are admonished to remember Lot's wife. Remembering Lot's wife is understanding that being captivated by your past bars you from moving in your direction of promise.

Sometimes I'm tempted to stop and look back at what I've left behind. But, the truth is, I've received clear instruction on the path forward and I refuse to turn to salt. The only option... the only direction I'm willing to move in ... is forward. Anything less would be uncivilized

Charmion Kinder

ENCOURAGEMENT FOR "THE MIDDLE"

"Get yourself ready! Stand up and say to them whatever I command you. Do not be terrified by them, or I will terrify you before them. Today I have made you a fortified city, an iron pillar and a bronze wall to stand against the whole land—against the kings of Judah, its officials, its priests and the people of the land. They will fight against you but will not overcome you, for I am with you and will rescue you," declares the LORD.

Jeremiah 1:17-19, NIV

I have a special attraction to this passage because it embodies the charge for enduring the arc of the journey, which for me can produce the toughest mental challenges. Starting can be easy. Finishing is a huge point of motivation. The middle can be an interesting and challenging juncture. There is an abundance of self-help books that I can find to help me start something. There are sermons to get me pretty amped up to finish strong, but it is in the middle where the enemy attacks our ability to see the finish line. The middle is where exhaustion sets in. It is because of this that some of us give up in the middle of the process.

There are some missteps and even some failures in life that we are going to have to push through because there is greatness on the other side. In the middle, we are vulnerable and if we are not careful we will quit and when we do that we deprive the world of our greatness. If we can just conquer that difficult midpoint that represents the "middle" of our process, greatness will be within your reach.

The prophet Jeremiah's story is a model for how to navigate that very difficult space called "the middle." Jeremiah was designed for a great purpose but his mandate was strategically eclipsed by many trials and challenges that he went through. He was attacked by his own brothers. He was beaten and put into the stocks by a priest and false prophet. He was imprisoned by the king and even threatened with death. Yet, God's personal message to Jeremiah was, "they can attack you but they will not overcome you." No matter how heavy or drawn out the preparation process may be, we have the ultimate ally that ensures our victorious finish.

None of us are exempt from difficulties. I have questioned why challenges are necessary for me to understand certain things. But I do know that God is a master at lessons, producing great things out of perseverance, and creating a deeper gratefulness that comes when we actually have to push through and are not given the goal automatically. As much as most teenagers would love to just try out the open road in a car after watching their parents drive, there is much more experience that has to happen before the honor of forward travel in a vehicle is bestowed. There are courses that must be taken and practical application performed before a license is earned and driving can begin.

Doesn't that sound like what life grants us in experience classes? How much more do we gain when we conquer the testing process?

To this end I declare that where I am is where I should be and I trust God for where I am going. Regardless of how it seems, the middle is not too hard. The future is too great." Commit to begin, conquer the middle, and have faith for the end!

Being defeated is often a temporary condition. Giving up is what makes it permanent

Marilyn Vos Savant

FASTING AND PRAYER

There, by the Ahava Canal, I proclaimed a fast, so that we might humble ourselves before our God and ask him for a safe journey for us and our children, with all our possessions. I was ashamed to ask the king for soldiers and horsemen to protect us from enemies on the road, because we had told the king, "The gracious hand of our God is on everyone who looks to him, but his great anger is against all who forsake him." So we fasted and petitioned our God about this, and he answered our prayer.

Ezra 8:21-23, NIV

Here Ezra, an Old Testament Priest, tells how he led a group of exiled Israelites back to Jerusalem after they were freed from Babylonian captivity. For Ezra, and the Israelites traveling with him, there was a long thousand-mile journey ahead. They were defenseless and traveling with their wives and children. Carrying all of their possessions, including gold and silver treasures, made them vulnerable to thieves. Ezra knew that this was not a journey he could lead on his own. He needed direction and a serious power injection. Ezra proclaimed a corporate fast to petition the Holy Spirit for both guidance and protection. Although this entire chapter is a valuable tool for the study of fasting and prayer, Ezra's summation here further illustrates its power. In Ezra 8:31, Ezra provides us with the end result: "The hand of our God was on us and he protected us from enemies and bandits along the way. So we arrived in Jerusalem."

My deepest desire is to possess the clarity of God's voice in my life. Like Ezra, I've found myself on roads to great destinations, but these roads were paved with vision thieves and enemies of distraction, fear and self-created roadblocks. Fasting has been my powerful hearing aid. It silences the noise and increases the volume of God's voice. By emptying myself of the baggage I didn't need for the journey, fasting prepared me for travel.

Fasting is so much more than refraining from food. It is deeper and the results are life changing. Fasting, by definition, is a deliberate and general abstention that demonstrates our level of commitment and our reach for God. Fasting is an act of willingness. It is a conscious choice to be uncomfortable in order to see God's power manifested in our lives. It is a focusing of our faith and a thoughtful commitment to turn our attention Godward. There are many different forms of fasting, including water fasts, juice fasts, sacrificing a particular meal daily, or fasting from people, things, and activities. Regardless of the fast you choose, the idea is to commit to denying yourself a particular pleasure. One year, I fasted from sports television during the month of March. Traditionally, I am glued to college basketball and March Madness is the pinnacle. That March fast proved to be a difficult sacrifice for me but it was a worthy one. For you, it may be going to the movies, shopping, social media, or even taking time off from communicating with a friend who you enjoy most.

In addition to the denial of pleasure, fasting must also be joined by a commitment to prayer and hearing from God. Be prepared for God to make changes in your life and reveal direction. Fasting increases our ability to hear God, so be intentional. Open the path of communication as frequently as possible. When you think of what you are fasting from, this is the time to pray. For example, if you are fasting from food, when you get hungry, read the Word of God, worship and pray. You will see an amazing difference in your results.

Like Ezra and the Israelites, you are traveling with the treasure of God's purpose for your life. You too need God's protection and guidance. I encourage you to make fasting and prayer a priority at every start of every new road. Anytime we are facing a major change in life, preparing to make an important decision, desire sanctification, or encountering a problem or hardship, we should do as Ezra did enter a fast. Ezra and his fellow travelers were rewarded with perfect safety the entire way. God honors fasting and prayer. When we use these as tools, we too have access to protection and guidance along roads uncertain.

Fasting confirms our utter dependence upon God by finding in Him a source of sustenance beyond food

Dallas Willard

DON'T SWEAT THE TECHNIQUE

But God's not finished. He's waiting around to be gracious to you. He's gathering strength to show mercy to you. God takes the time to do everything right—everything.

Isaiah 30:18, MSG

I am a nightmare in the hair salon chair. I know how I want my hair to look so I am quick to pick up a mirror and make evaluations along the way. I am the client who has to make sure that the job is being done in the right way. From the washing bowl all the way to the curling iron, I ask all kinds of questions. One Saturday, I was sitting with my veteran hair stylist and making suggestions, critiquing the process until she literally pulled the mirror from my hand and proceeded to read me my rights. She said, "If at the end you don't like it, I will change it. But, I know what I am doing and I will make sure that your hair is right. Until then, sit there, relax and let me work. I am not done."

What a Word.

How many times have I critiqued God's unfinished work? How many times have I inserted my way over His, even when God has proven that He knows best? How many times have I questioned the "how" although I had faith in the "what?"

We are works in progress and God knows exactly what He is doing. I sometimes feel too comfortable telling God how things should work. My prayer time is occasionally similar to my hair salon experience: "God, do I really have to wait until I am married? I get the whole relationship that pleases God leading to marriage, but You know statistics say that people with healthy sex lives are much happier. I might have a better temperament in managing my relationship if I get some…. Father, is it truly necessary for me to tithe for You to open the windows of heaven and pour me out a blessing? I really need to pay for a few immediate needs that fall under other commandments. Can obedience in this area be transferred?"

Sounds pretty ridiculous, doesn't it? Well, I am guilty as charged. It's like clay jumping off of a spinning wheel and telling the potter "I got this. I know how I should be made so you should try this method..." I am not going to consult Jay-Z on how to write lyrics for his next album and I surely am not going to consult my gynecologist on how to give a pap smear. So, I should feel equally uncomfortable trying to advise God on how to guide my life toward His divine purpose. Just like in the area of hair care, and in the previous examples, I have nowhere near the level of expertise for such consultation. Therefore, I have to tell myself, "Fall back and have faith in God's preferred process, Halleemah."

If I know that all things work for my good (Romans 8:28) then I must also know that there is purpose even in the things that don't happen in the way we would like. If I am confident that He who began a good work in me will carry it on to completion until the day of Christ Jesus (Philippians 1:6) then I should place equal confidence in God's preferred method of finishing the work He started. God is not done. Sit in the chair and let Him create His work of art.

"For my thoughts are not your thoughts, neither are your ways my ways," declares the LORD. As the heavens are higher than the earth, so are my ways higher than your ways and my thoughts than your thoughts."

ISAIAH 55:8-9, NIV

POWER OF PRESENCE

For I decided that while I was with you I would forget everything except Jesus Christ, the one who was crucified. I came to you in weakness—timid and trembling.

1 Corinthians 2:2-3, NLT

The healing of communities, through the power of presence and relationship, was a concept that I believe God wanted me to see at the apex to my seminary experience.

While I was in graduate school, I traveled with a group of medical and theology students to Haiti with hopes of building relationships, providing medical assistance and exploring healing in developing countries. The focus of this trip was building relationships and providing culturally relevant assistance to people living in extreme poverty. Haiti, for me, and for many, was as extreme as it got. In 2002, eighty countries were ranked in the category of competitiveness and the United States, where I was traveling from, was ranked number one. Haiti, where I was traveling to, was ranked number eighty. I was going from one space to a completely different one.

Traveling to Haiti gave me, and many others, the chance to leave the many comforts that we are afforded and be present, in a completely different context, for eight days. We participated in medical clinics, visited schools, served in churches, spent time with the sick, and sat in on roundtable discussions regarding investment opportunities and ways that we could add value to Haiti from our homes in the United States.

Healing, in the context of poverty, requires us to be willing to instill worth in others, listen and learn, be willing to receive, and serve while encouraging with humility. This was a difficult task, especially because many of us were itching to do something or see some tangible results. But, I had to learn what it really meant to participate in a ministry of presence.

I have learned to never underestimate the power of presence and never underestimate the power of what I perceived to be a miniscule gift. I could not heal their diseases. I could not cure their poverty in that short-term mission trip, but I could hold someone's hand. I could pray the Lord's Prayer with them, and I could comb a child's hair. I will never know how much certain acts may mean to a person. But, I do understand the power of presence. We minimize some of the greatest acts of love when we use language like, "I *just* did this" or "well, I was *only* there for eight days." There is power in simply being present with people. It lets them know that there is love for them in the world.

"My own desire to be useful, to do something significant, or to be part of some impressive project is so strong that soon my time is taken up by

meetings, conferences, study groups, and workshops that prevent me from walking the streets. It is difficult not to have plans, not to organize people around an urgent cause, and not to feel that you are working directly for social progress. But I wonder more and more if the first thing shouldn't be to know people by name, to eat and drink with them, to listen to their stories and tell your own, and to let them know with words, handshakes, and hugs that you do not simply like them, but truly love them."

Henri Nouwen

TIME MINDFULNESS

See then that you walk circumspectly, not as fools but as wise, redeeming the time, because the days are evil. Therefore do not be unwise, but understand what the will of the Lord is.

Ephesians 5:15-17, NKJV

Time management speaks to how purposeful we are with our time and as much as this concept is used in school and in business settings, it is also a scriptural principle.

Paul in Ephesians 5 admonishes us to not take for granted the time we have and to use it wisely. It pleases God and helps us to be aware of His presence when we carefully steward His gift of time. Time is our most precious asset and greatest resource; however, it can also be the most neglected and ignored. As angry as I get about people who waste my time (biggest pet peeve) I am becoming more cognizant of ways that I am guilty of the same fault.

Every increment of time is valuable and I am becoming more conscious about how I spend it. I specifically pay close attention to the small moments that make up my "spare" time. The small five or ten minute increments in between meetings, waking up and getting in the shower, and even sitting on the train or awaiting an appointment are moments spent ineffectively when they can be utilized with more intention.

How do I use short increments of time? Taking an account in this area helped me identify weaknesses in how I used my spare time. I found that I was more prone to spend these moments idly than to put them to use. Using spare moments more deliberately led to a radical increase in my productivity, energy, and ability to balance.

When I get home from a long workday, instead of turning on the news or Sports Center first, I put on soft music and spend 5 minutes completely still in meditation to come down from my day. During my mid day breaks, I try to spend the lunch hour in fellowship with other people instead of working through lunch while eating. I also have begun to do more with my mornings. I picked up "What the Most Successful People Do Before Breakfast: A Short Guide to Making Over Your Mornings-and Life" by Laura Vanderkam and applied a few tips. Instead of scrolling through social media when I wake up and have additional time before my workout, I sometimes replace the cover of my phone screen with a post it note that reads, "PRAY." This also gave me brief moments of prayer time throughout the day.

These activities are certainly an effort in progress, but they are exercises to aid me in my commitment to spending spare moments with intentionality.

We are called to be good stewards of our time. I am learning to seek God's will in the small, spare moments of life. God's will is not limited to the overall purpose of our journey here on earth, but it can also be found in the activities that make up the finite amount of time in each day.

Guard well your spare moments. They are like uncut diamonds. Discard them and their value will never be known. Improve them and they will become the brightest gems in a useful life.

Ralph Waldo Emerson

EPILOGUE

Throughout this book you have seen me write about world travel and incredible accomplishments. You have seen a thread of wins and mountaintop experiences but the truth is, it would take a whole other book to show you the amount of losses, mistakes, and failed attempts that proceeded. If I had the time, I would write about the times I had to grow up quickly. How, in middle school, I did homework in Leuder's Park under the Rosecrans' streetlight when the life that waited for me at home was overwhelming. You would read about the terrible decisions I made due to my own vulnerability and need to be a people pleaser. The times that I had no money and no one to call for it, would be a common theme on these pages. So frequent that I often went to pond shops when I couldn't ask for help with my car note. I would open up about the times I made relationship choices out of insecurity and loneliness. And all the scholarships and jobs I applied for and didn't receive. Or, I'd list all of the doors that were slammed in my face and all of the *no* responses I heard before there was ever a *maybe* let alone a *yes*. I could write pages and pages of these experiences.

But, my hope is that you might see Christ's deliverance in my life and His righteous hand covering me all the way to those hilltops of high education, spiritual breakthroughs, growth, and success. That you might see the humility that comes with understanding that our righteousness is as filthy rags but we are also a royal priesthood. We are servants of the Lord but we are also called His friend. My hope is that you might see the symmetry of these truths. And that in these pages you might see Him and take the opportunity to know Him for yourself in a balanced way.

Here's to your endless summer.

ACKNOWLEDGEMENTS

To the "Seven" – Courtney, Kaishelle, Ebony, Rochelle, Precious, Tameka, and Kirstyn- You ladies all ride so hard for me. You are in these pages. And you worked tirelessly to build the platform that I've mounted. "Love's too weak to define, just what you mean to me."

To my baby sis Rachel and girls who've become my sisters – Michelle Webb, Dacquiri, Malaysia, Chasity, LaTanya, Nichole Kirtley, Shawna, Pascale, Brianna, Courtnee, Michelle Stewart, Crystal, Karan, Krystyna, and the Boo Gang. Some for ten years some for one, but you are all so very special to me.

To Donte Brown for being the first person to dare me to do something great. I will love you forever. Rest in peace.

To my immediate and extended family I love each of you! Curt, I am so proud of you. Teaching! Keep rising above your challenges. There is a level of greatness that awaits you. Anthony, its amazing having you home. Eighteen years away can harden a man but you refused to settle for anything less than life at its best. Look at you traveling the country now. Limitless. Granddad, thanks for loving me selflessly and unconditionally. It taught me how to do the same.

To my brothers who didn't come from my mom but you are the definition of the word. Dave Parks, Jairus, McBride, J Tanner, Feezy, Armond, Josh, Shumate, Deng, Darrel, Salim, I'd jump in front of a moving bus to protect you if it ever came to it. 143.

To the beautiful little girl whom I am honored to co-Godmother, Kendall Parks. The thought of your potential inspires me to be a woman that you can be proud of. My hope is that my work blazes a trail for you in some way.

To the young ladies that I've been blessed to mentor over the years Jordan, Kelly, Marvi, Annie, Chloe– you remind me so frequently of why it's so important to live a life poured out. You honor me with every hurdle that you face and clear with fearless ambition and the will to succeed.

To the amazing women who've attended my bible studies in DC, Durham, and on those Chicago rooftops – thanks for encouraging me to expand the reach of these messages.

To my team at Legacy Venture Consulting –volunteers, project staff, and all of the clients and charitable athletes that I've worked with- you have made me a better executive. Thank you for your service to this world through sport.

To my pastoral covering – Bishop Kenneth Ulmer of Faithful Central and Pastor Charles Jenkins of Fellowship Missionary Baptist Church – you are more than Shepherds. Thank you for your love and leadership.

To the community of faith leaders that I learned alongside while at Duke Div, thank you for your service all around the world. You motivate me with the diversity of ways you work to be Gods hands and feet in this world. Black, White, Republican, Democrat, Blue Devil, Tarheel, southern born or Cali tattooed, we are all joined by the cross.

To Dom Kennedy and Kendall Hurns for inspiring me to produce my best work independently and from the heart - embracing that as my definition of success. This is my mixtape. And to Kristin Williams of FAME Production Group for being my producer. Genius entrepreneurial hustlas ya'll are.

To Compton, CA – the city I adore. Every accomplishment is a tribute to you and the potential on your corners.

To Howard University, I owe you so much more than I could ever really give. There's a sense that as alumni we have work to do to fulfill the honor of graduating from Howard U. And with every step it's my earnest intent.

ABOUT THE AUTHOR

Halleemah Nash is a leader in multiple facets of inspirational engagement with specific experience in ministry and managing high profile, sport affiliated charitable entities.

Nash was ordained at Fellowship Missionary Baptist Church in Chicago, Illinois. Shortly after her ordination, she was appointed Youth Pastor, where she served for two years, and has continued as a guest speaker. To expand ministry opportunities outside of the church, Halleemah launched a series of women's bible studies for working professionals.`

Believing in the power of sport to create social change, Nash launched her own philanthropy consulting firm Legacy Venture Consulting, where she has developed opportunities for clients in the NBA, NFL, NHL, and university athletic programs.

Halleemah has also served as a speaker or panels, workshops, keynote addresses, commencements, and corporate engagements throughout the United States and abroad. As a motivational speaker, she shares her story of overcoming adversity and her journey in finding purpose through a life of service. Her story of triumph has connected her with audiences across racial, socioeconomic, and geographic boundaries.

Her work in ministry and philanthropy has been featured in Rolling Out, Chicago Sun Times, Michigan Avenue and Marie Claire Magazine, NPR radio, ABC, and NBC.

Originally from Compton, California Halleemah Nash received a Bachelor of Business Administration from Howard University School of Business, a Master of Divinity and a Certificate in Non-Profit Management from Duke University and a Certificate in Sports Philanthropy from George Washington University.

www.HalleemahNash.com

Made in the USA
Lexington, KY
23 November 2015